✪ WEAPONS OF WAR
SMALL ARMS
1870–1950

✪ WEAPONS OF WAR
SMALL ARMS
1870–1950

CHARTWELL
BOOKS

CHARTWELL BOOKS
an imprint of Book Sales
a division of Quarto Publishing Group USA Inc.
142 West 36th Street, 4th Floor
New York, New York 10018
USA

Contributing authors: Chris Chant, Steve Crawford, Martin J. Dougherty, Ian Hogg,
Robert Jackson, Chris McNab, Michael Sharpe, Philip Trewhitt

ISBN 978-0-7858-3155-6

Printed in China

PICTURE CREDITS
Photographs:
Art-Tech/Aerospace: 18, 20–23
Art-Tech/MARS: 7, 17
Cody Images: 8–16, 19

Illustrations: © Art-Tech/Aerospace

CONTENTS

Introduction

Early Automatics

Weapons design was revolutionised in the late nineteenth century with the development of the magazine loading system.

The true revolution in weapons design must reside in the 19th century. Johann Nikolaus Dreyse's Zündnadelgewehr (needle gun) and Alphonse Chassepot's Fusil d'Infanterie Modèle 1866 established the basic design of the bolt-action rifle, while later in the century designers such as the Frenchman Basile Gras, the Austrian Ferdinand Mannlicher and the German Peter Paul Mauser would ally the bolt-action with magazine loading systems. Hand-cranked machine guns such as the Mitrailleuse and the Gatling, the latter with a 3000 rounds per minute (rpm) rate of fire, were already showing their destructive possibilities.

More significantly, landmark figures, such as Hiram Stevens Maxim and Baron Odkolek von Augezd respectively, applied to machine guns the principles of recoil and gas operation which are used to this day. The Maxim gun, in particular, spread around the world and proved its hideous efficiency when used by the British in Africa and Afghanistan in the 1890s.

In the world of the handgun, the 19th century was also a time of exceptional progress. After Samuel Colt brought his percussion revolver onto the market in 1835, and Horace Smith and Daniel B. Wesson introduced the first cartridge revolver, the pistol became a viable combat weapon. Double-action (meaning that the gun is cocked and fired in a single pull of the trigger), ejection rod emptying of cylinder cases and side-opening cylinders quickly followed; barring metallurgical limits and some technical sophistications, the revolvers of the late 19th century could claim a capability little different from the handguns of today. In addition, designers such as Hugo Bochardt were already introducing the automatic, magazine-loaded pistol – a form that would overtake the revolver in popularity in the 20th century.

Combine the progress in gun design with the allied fact that the 19th century gave us the true unitary cartridge and more efficient nitro-cellulose propellants, and the 20th century may seem to play second fiddle. However, whereas the 19th century was perhaps the age of the greater experimentation, the 20th was the century in which experiment would give way to excellence.

THE NEW CENTURY

From the turn of the century forward, modern military men were becoming increasingly aware of the advancing technology that confronted them on land and sea and in the air. Nowhere was the profound effect of man's ingenuity more dramatically proved than on the battlefield. The repeating rifle had given way to the improved bolt-action

MAUSER GEWEHR 98: see page 72

The Mauser Gewehr 98 provided the prototype for many other rifle designs of the era.

shoulder arms of Mauser, Lee-Enfield, Springfield and others, and in turn the semiautomatic rifle had emerged in the mid-1930s with the introduction of the M1 Garand. By 1944, US general George S. Patton Jr. (1885–1945) had commented that the Garand was the 'greatest battle implement ever devised'.

Without doubt, the generation of firearms designers that altered, improved and generally revised the rifles of the years prior to World War I were influenced by a legion of innovators and designers who had gone before them. The Mauser line can claim descendants around the world, for

example, and many of the rifles that were fielded by armies of World War II trace their components to the Mauser Gewehr 98, the forerunner of the Karabiner 98k standard issue rifle of the Wehrmacht from the 1930s until the end of World War II. More than 14 million examples of the K98k were manufactured in the decade from 1935 to 1945.

TESTED IN FIRE

World War I can be seen as the point in history when the old ways of individuated war were swept away by the industrialised destruction brought by new firearms

WEAPONS OF WAR

HOTCHKISS MODEL 1914: see page 142

WEAPONS OF WAR

MAXIM MASCHINENGEWEHR '08: see page 134

WEAPONS OF WAR

VICKERS MK 1: see page 139

The machine gun reaped a harvest of death like no other weapon in the history of warfare.

technologies. Effective bolt-action rifles were now in the hands of all soldiers, and a two-man machine-gun team could deliver the firepower previously held by an entire company. The smokeless propellants now used converted almost all their explosive energy into gas, thus giving rifles the high velocities needed to kill at ranges of 1000m- (3280ft-) plus, while remaining hidden. Firepower was now superior to manpower, as was illustrated when, at Mons in August 1914, the 7500 men of the British Expeditionary Force, armed with Lee-Enfield rifles and limited numbers of Vickers machine guns, stopped the advance of 200,000 soldiers of the German 1st Army.

Perhaps no other infantry-level weapon has illustrated the tragic failure of military tactics to keep pace with advancing technology more than the machine gun, which proliferated during World War I. Reaping a harvest of death like no other small arms in history, machine guns fired from entrenched positions killed infantrymen with reckless abandon during the war of attrition in the trenches. In the summer of 1916, British sergeant Charles Quinnell faced German machine guns on the Western Front

COLT M1911: see page 41

and lived to tell of his horrifying ordeal. 'The first wave were down,' he remembered. 'Two machine guns played on them and they were completely wiped out. Everybody was either killed or wounded. We went through. We got halfway across [no-man's-land] and then the machine guns found us and they played on us like spraying with a hose. At the finish I was the only one standing.'

The consequence of these technologies was that troop exposure on open ground became suicidal. Thus, military tactics shifted to become more defensive in nature, employing groundworks, trenches and fortifications. Although such defensive tactics had already been seen in the South African War (1899–1902) and the Russo-Japanese War (1904–1905), World War I shifted them to a previously unimaginable scale. As so often happens in weapons development, the conditions imposed by new firearms created the need for new tactics, which in turn produced new weapons to support those tactics.

By 1916, German forces were employing Sturmtruppe – small groups of heavily armed shock troops that would puncture sections of enemy trenches following a short, intense artillery bombardment. In the confines of trenches, wielding a 1.25m- (49.2in) long Mauser Gewehr 98 bolt-action rifle was awkward, its five-round magazine was inadequate and its long-range power was unwarranted. Two new types of small arm were born – the submachine gun and the light machine gun.

BROWNING HP 1935: see page 58

LUGER (PARABELLUM P'08): see page 37

The submachine gun answered the needs of trench warfare by providing full automatic fire using pistol-calibre cartridges, usually the ubiquitous 9mm Parabellum, to make the recoil manageable, and had a convenient length and weight for the trench confines. Range was limited – about 30–40m (98–131ft) – but more than adequate for most actual combat distances. The first submachine gun was Italian: the Vilar-Perosa was a blowback weapon set in a double-barrel configuration with a cyclic rate of fire of 1200rpm.

Although designed for Austrian Alpine troops, it was actually too heavy for convenient personal use and was more suited to being mounted on vehicles and in aircraft. By contrast, the German Bergmann MP18 was a reliable, powerful 9mm weapon, purposely designed for trench-clearing operations. It was an excellent gun and proved popular with the German shock troops; and the submachine gun would become a fundamental type of infantry weapon for the next three decades.

The light machine gun originated out of a similar impulse towards more mobile firepower. Heavy machine guns such as the Vickers, Maxim and Schwarzlose were incredibly weighty when fully armed and assembled on their tripod unit. A Maxim ready for firing could weigh around 62kg (137lb) which, although light enough to be manhandled by a team, still lacked the portability to act as a forward-support weapon during assaults. The answer was the light machine gun, introduced from about 1915. Light enough to be carried by one man, these guns were usually gas-operated, air-cooled

BREN GUN: see page 166

THOMPSON M1928: see page 100–101

WEAPONS OF WAR

STEN MK II: see page 119

weapons which could be quickly set up and fired from a bipod. For convenience, they tended to use a magazine rather than belt feed. Significant examples were the British Lewis Gun, the US M1918 Browning Automatic Rifle (BAR), the Hotchkiss Mle 1909, the German MG'08/15, and such weapons dramatically increased the weight of fire that could be brought to bear during assaults.

The pistol was also a natural favourite for trench combat, and, by World War I, pistol development was centring on the automatic pistol. Classics such as John Browning's famous M1911 and George Luger's Pistole '08 had already entered service, and self-loading pistols by Beretta, Savage, Webley & Scott, and Mauser were making an impact.

Usually operating by blowback or short recoil, automatic pistols had the advantage of holding more rounds than a revolver's cylinder and, usually, offered a more convenient loading method through a detachable magazine or a charger of rounds inserted into an internal magazine.

INTERWAR DEVELOPMENTS

The end of World War I left military strategists with many important tactical lessons, not least of which was the greater value of short-range portable firepower for infantry combat than long-range guns. Thus the interwar period continued the development of the light- and submachine gun form, although the bolt-action rifle would continue as the main infantry weapon for most nations until at least the end of World War II (Japan, in particular, lagged behind).

The interwar period and, later, World War II did, however, take the technologies of the machine gun in all its forms to new heights. To list the wartime submachine guns – weapons such as the German MP38/40, the British Sten, the Soviet PPSh41, and the US

PPSh-41: see page 113

M1 GARAND: see page 85

Industrialised production methods using steel pressings and stampings became integral to the success of any weapon design during World War II.

M3 and Thompson – is to perform a roll call for some of the most famous firearms ever invented. Yet the conditions of mass mobile warfare imposed by German blitzkrieg meant that war had to be fought on the production lines as well as on the battlefields. Thus industrialised production methods using steel pressings and stampings became integral to any successful weapon design in World War II. The Soviet PPSh41, for example, was simple enough to produce even in small rural workshops and consequently it was possible to keep Soviet forces stocked with this invaluable source of firepower.

Major advances in production and sophistication of machine guns were also taking place. While some, such as the estimable Browning M2HB, were making reputations that would keep them in use for the next half century, World War II was the period in which the general purpose machine gun reached its apotheosis. Two German examples, in particular – the MG34 and MG42 – demonstrated such high rates of fire, dependability, range and general killing force that they questioned the relevance of heavy machine guns at all. The success of such weapons in mobile support roles was such

MG42: see page 171

BROWNING M2HB: see page 150–151

that many are with us today in forms such as the German M3.

WORLD WAR II

World War II was a watershed in 20th century weapons design not only for the quality (and quantity) of machine gun technology which emerged, but also for the introduction of a new weapon form that remains, to this day, the central infantry firearm of all major armies – the self-loading automatic rifle. Although the Russian Vladimir Fyodorov had created a 6.5mm automatic rifle during World War II, it was the US M1 Garand that established itself as the first significant self-loading rifle, although it retained the full rifle calibre .30-06 round. The true assault rifle

was designed from the recognition that the standard high-power rifles of the day had a range far in excess of the average 400m (1297ft) distance at which men fought. In response, the visionary Hugo Schmeisser designed the Sturmgewehr (assault rifle) 44 in 1941. Looking ultra-modern for the time, this was a gas-operated weapon. The long, curved magazine held thirty 7.92 x 33mm 'Kurz' (Short) cartridges, which were the same calibre as Mauser rifle rounds, but with reduced power for more range-realistic usage and controllability at full automatic.

Accuracy, endurance and firepower were the three pillars on which a successful rifle was built, and the crucible of war provided a proving ground for design innovation.

STURMGEWEHR 44: see page 90

From the Sturmgewehr 44 rose the iconic Kalashnikov AK-47 assault rifle, the US-made M16 and other such weapons that shaped the future of warfare.

Thus between 1939 and 1945, the bolt-action rifle of a half-century earlier was fighting alongside the semiautomatic and fully automatic rifles that would dominate the battlefield into the twenty-first century. With the end of World War II, most major powers were starting to recognise that the assault rifle would become the best infantry weapon, situated as it was between the pistol-calibre, short-range submachine gun and the long-range rifle.

In 1947, the most famous assault rifle of all time was produced by Mikhail Timofeyevich Kalashnikov – the AK-47. It fired a 7.62mm intermediate cartridge and impressed the world with its ability to deliver heavy individual firepower while enduring the worst battlefield conditions.

Webley Bulldog

The Webley Bulldog was a stocky little revolver which was produced by Webley from the late 1870s, and whose durability as a firearm took it into the 20th century, if only in service rather than in production. It was developed from an earlier Webley revolver produced for the Royal Irish Constabulary, and first arrived on the scene in .442in calibre, then went to .45in, then to .32in. Whatever the calibre, each Bulldog could be relied upon to deliver workable firepower for its user from its five-chamber cylinder. The guns were also cheap, and a combination of good price and solidity made the Bulldog a popular weapon which became widely distributed. The main problem with the Bulldog was that its very short barrel – only 53mm (2.1in) – which gave it an acutely compressed effective range of around 15m (49ft).

SPECIFICATIONS

COUNTRY OF ORIGIN UK
CALIBRE .32in British
LENGTH 140mm (5.5in)
WEIGHT 0.31kg (0.7lb)
BARREL 53mm (2.1in)
FEED/MAGAZINE CAPACITY 5-round cylinder
OPERATION Revolver
MUZZLE VELOCITY 190mps (625fps)
EFFECTIVE RANGE 15m (49ft)

Chamelot-Delvigne 1874

The Chamelot-Delvigne was a Belgian weapon designed by Joseph Camelot and Henri-Gustave Delvigne which went on to become a standard French army pistol during the latter years of the 19th and early years of the 20th century. The series of guns actually emerged in 1865 but it was not until a new version was produced in 1871 that export sales increased. In 1873 an 11mm version was produced which was taken into service by the French cavalry. Early versions of this weapon were hampered by a chronically under-powered cartridge which limited what was a solid and reliable gun. This problem was eventually cleared with a new cartridge which offered nearly double the power, and for this round the 1874/90 version was produced. In this form, the Chamelot-Delvigne served French and other European troops into World War I.

SPECIFICATIONS

COUNTRY OF ORIGIN France/Belgium
CALIBRE 11mm
LENGTH 240mm (9.4in)
WEIGHT 1.08kg (2.3lb)
BARREL 114mm (4.49in)
FEED/MAGAZINE CAPACITY 6-round cylinder
OPERATION Revolver
MUZZLE VELOCITY 183mps (600fps)
EFFECTIVE RANGE 20m (66ft)

Mauser Zig-Zag

The Mauser Zig-Zag was one of a series of Mauser weapons which emerged during the latter years of the 19th century and influenced the weapons of the 20th by either service or design. The most noticeable feature of these guns were their mechanism for revolving the cylinder during firing. This consisted of a set of grooves machined into the outer wall of the cylinder, into which a stud attached to the mainspring carrier was located. Thus, as the trigger was pulled, the movement of the mainspring carrier and stud was directed into the grooves and the cylinder revolved round to the next chamber for firing. The positioning of the grooves ensured that the chamber was correctly aligned for each firing. Mauser Zig-Zags came in solid and hinge-frame versions, with some (as pictured here) having the feature of simultaneous cartridge ejection via a rod located beneath the barrel.

SPECIFICATIONS
COUNTRY OF ORIGIN Germany
CALIBRE 10.9mm
LENGTH 298mm (11.75in)
WEIGHT 1.19kg (2.6lb)
BARREL 165mm (6.5in)
FEED/MAGAZINE CAPACITY 6-round cylinder
OPERATION Revolver
MUZZLE VELOCITY 198mps (650fps)
EFFECTIVE RANGE 30m (98ft)

Smith & Wesson Double-Action

After some four years of research, during the 1880s, Smith & Wesson advanced its range of gun designs with a new series of double-action revolvers (i.e. revolvers that can be fired through both a single pull on the trigger which takes the hammer through its full cycle, or by manually cocking the hamer then releasing it through a shortened trigger pull). Using the break-open system of ejection and reloading with the barrel section hinged in front of the cylinder, they were popular and reliable guns that fired Smith &Wesson's .38 bullet to an effective range of around 20m (66ft). The double-action range was proficient enough to endure beyond the 19th century to the 1940s, during which time side-opening cylinder weapons became more prevalent in weapon design and eventually superseded break-open guns.

SPECIFICATIONS
COUNTRY OF ORIGIN USA
CALIBRE .38 S&W
LENGTH 190mm (7.5in)
WEIGHT 0.51kg (1.12lb)
BARREL 83mm (3.27in), 5 grooves, rh
FEED/MAGAZINE CAPACITY 6-round cylinder
OPERATION Revolver
MUZZLE VELOCITY 190mps (625fps)
EFFECTIVE RANGE 20m (66ft)

Bochardt C/93

Produced as it was at the end of the 19th century, the Bochardt C/93 was a significant step forwards towards an effective self-loading pistol, though it was quickly surpassed by the likes of Mauser and Bergmann. It was a large and heavy weapon with a distinctive 'fishing reel' appearance on account of its toggle-lock system of locking. This was borrowed from the Maxim machine gun, and the C/93 used a similar short-recoil principle of operation. Perhaps the most significant advance in the Bochardt handgun was that it went from charger loading into a fixed magazine to using a detachable 8-round box magazine, which was inserted in the bottom of the pistol grip in the way that has now become familiar. The C/93's production ceased in 1898, but it served into the twentieth century, often fitted with a shoulder stock to allow it to act as a carbine.

SPECIFICATIONS

COUNTRY OF ORIGIN Germany
CALIBRE 7.65mm
LENGTH 279mm (11in)
WEIGHT 1.1kg (2.56lb)
BARREL 165.1mm (6.5in), 4 grooves, rh
FEED/MAGAZINE CAPACITY 8-round detachable box magazine
OPERATION Short recoil
MUZZLE VELOCITY 326mps (1070fps)
EFFECTIVE RANGE 20m (65.6ft)

Meiji Revolver

The Meiji revolver, or the Meiji 26 Nen Shiki Kenju, to give it its full name, was produced in the last years of the 19th century as part of Japan's general attempt to catch up with the rest of the Western industrialised world in terms of arms manufacture. Japan's relative inexperience in this field perhaps shows in the design, with borrowings from Smith & Wesson, Gasser and Nagant which seem to inform the pistol's construction. The Meiji was a double-action only revolver, and proved to be a rather inadequate gun for service, being both inaccurate and tending towards unreliability. It was .35in in calibre and used a break-open cylinder for reloading. Cartridge ejection was performed by an automatic ejector. The Meiji did not match the quality of the guns it imitated, yet it was still put into service in large numbers across Japan.

SPECIFICATIONS
COUNTRY OF ORIGIN Japan
CALIBRE 9mm
LENGTH 235mm (9.25in)
WEIGHT 0.91kg (2lb)
BARREL 119mm (4.7in)
FEED/MAGAZINE CAPACITY 6-round cylinder
OPERATION Revolver
MUZZLE VELOCITY 246mps (750fps)
EFFECTIVE RANGE 30m (91ft)

Nagant M1895

Although the Nagant M1895 was produced, as its name reveals, in the late 19th century while Russia still had a Tsar, it continued in service until the 1950s with the Soviet Union and was a remarkable weapon. Its most significant contribution to weapon history is that it used a means of completely eradicating the fractional loss of gas pressure between the cylinder and barrel common to the vast majority of revolvers. It achieved this by pushing the cylinder forwards onto the tapered barrel end when the hammer was cocked, which in turn allowed the long Nagant cartridge, which held the bullet entirely in its case length, to enter directly into the barrel and produce complete obduration on firing. The Nagant's long service record is a testimony to the success of this procedure and it was a prized weapon for many years.

SPECIFICATIONS
COUNTRY OF ORIGIN USSR/Russia
CALIBRE 7.62 x 38R Russian Revolver
LENGTH 203mm (8in)
WEIGHT 0.89kg (1.96lb)
BARREL 114mm (4.5in), 6 grooves, rh
FEED/MAGAZINE CAPACITY 7 rounds
OPERATION Single- or double-action revolver
MUZZLE VELOCITY 305mps (1000fps)
EFFECTIVE RANGE 30m (98ft)

Webley-Fosbery

The Webley-Fosbery's appearance as a conventional revolver belies its revolutionary, albeit inefficient, operation as a halfway house between a revolver and an automatic pistol. It was designed by Colonel G. V. Fosbery VC in the mid-1890s and it would stay in service with the British armed forces until the end of World War I. On firing the Webley-Fosbery, the barrel and cylinder would recoil along a slide on the top of the butt and trigger system. This would recock the hammer, while a stud on the slide engaged with grooves on the cylinder to turn the cylinder to the next round. Despite its ingenuity, the Webley-Fosbery was an unwieldy weapon which was hard to control on firing and vulnerable to dirt – something that was hardly in short supply on the Western Front. By 1915, production of it had ceased.

SPECIFICATIONS

COUNTRY OF ORIGIN UK
CALIBRE .455in British Service
LENGTH 279mm (11in)
WEIGHT 1.25kg (1.378lb)
BARREL 152mm (6in), 7 grooves, rh
FEED/MAGAZINE CAPACITY 6 rounds
OPERATION Automatic revolver
MUZZLE VELOCITY 183mps (600fps)
EFFECTIVE RANGE 30m (98ft)

Bergmann 1896

Bergmann started producing automatic pistols in 1894 in a variety of calibres including 5mm, 6.5mm and 8mm. These experiments were a little precarious to say the least, owing to an extraction method which involved the spent case ricocheting off the new round sitting behind it. The 1896, however, used a more standard extractor, and thus had enough success to keep it in work into the twentieth century. It was lighter in weight than many other self-loading pistols of the time, and was also compact enough for genuine useability. Loading to the integral magazine was done via an access plate on the magazine which was released by catch just in front of the trigger guard. Bergmann quickly superseded the 1896 model handgun with new designs and went on to produce some seminal firearms during the 20th century.

SPECIFICATIONS
COUNTRY OF ORIGIN Germany
CALIBRE 7.63mm
LENGTH 245mm (9.6in)
WEIGHT 1.13kg (2.5lb)
BARREL 102mm (4in)
FEED/MAGAZINE CAPACITY 5-round integral box magazine
OPERATION Blowback
MUZZLE VELOCITY 380mps (1250fps)
EFFECTIVE RANGE 30m (98ft)

Browning Model 1900

The long-standing association between John M. Browning and the Belgian arms manufacturer Fabrique Nationale d'Armes de Guerre (FN) led to the production of many classic firearms in the 20th century. The first of these was the Browning Modèle 1900, which was conceived in the late 19th century and went into service in 1900. It was a blowback pistol which set itself apart by having a recoil spring sited above the barrel that acted not only in recoil action, but also as the firing pin spring. The gun was an all-round success in terms of design, and some one million were produced in total. These were much used by military forces across the world – although usually without offical status, as the turn of the century was still a period of adjustment to the idea of the automatic pistol, and revolvers were seen as being more reliable weapons.

SPECIFICATIONS

COUNTRY OF ORIGIN Belgium
CALIBRE 7.65mm Browning (.32 ACP)
LENGTH 170mm (6.75in)
WEIGHT 0.62kg (1.37lb)
BARREL 101mm (4in), 6 grooves, rh
FEED/MAGAZINE CAPACITY 7-round detachable box magazine
OPERATION Blowback
MUZZLE VELOCITY 290mps (950fps)
EFFECTIVE RANGE 30m (98ft)

Mannlicher Model 1901

The Model 1901 was the first of a series of Mannlicher firearms produced by the well-known Austrian manufacturer Steyr between 1901 and 1905, although the first Mannlicher pistol was actually produced in 1900 by Von Dreyse. All the pistols were quality weapons, even if both their commercial and their military success were limited. Two features distinguish the M1901. First, the delayed-blowback operation worked on a system in which the delay was imposed by a spring-and-cam system restraining the slide during its rearward travel. Secondly, the Mannlicher guns have an integral magazine which is loaded by pushing a charger of cartridges down through the open slide. One of the biggest markets for the guns was the Argentine Army, and the 7.63mm ammunition still remains in production in South America today.

SPECIFICATIONS

COUNTRY OF ORIGIN Austria
CALIBRE 7.63 x 21mm Mannlicher
LENGTH 246mm (9.68in)
WEIGHT 0.91kg (2lb)
BARREL 157mm (6.18in), 4 grooves, rh
FEED/MAGAZINE CAPACITY 8-round integral box magazine
OPERATION Delayed blowback
MUZZLE VELOCITY 312mps (1024fps)
EFFECTIVE RANGE 30m (98ft)

Colt Police Positive

The Police Positive range of Colt revolvers began life in 1905, a development from the earlier range of Pocket Positive revolvers which had achieved popularity in the United States. Throughout its production life the gun was issued in a wide variety of different calibres to suit different roles, and the barrel lengths also fluctuated from a target version (specifications below) to snub nose versions. The virtue of the Police Positive range was primarily that of most Colt handguns – they worked and were capable of taking a man down (early models suffered from a lack of power which was amended by the introduction of a new S&W .38 round). They were also light and were balanced in firing. Police Positive guns or their derivations remained in production into the 1960s, and their design heritage is still influential today.

SPECIFICATIONS

COUNTRY OF ORIGIN USA
CALIBRE 0.22in
LENGTH 260mm (10.25in)
WEIGHT 0.68kg (1.5lb)
BARREL 152mm (6in)
FEED/MAGAZINE CAPACITY 6-round cylinder
OPERATION Revolver
MUZZLE VELOCITY 354mps (1161fps)
EFFECTIVE RANGE 30m (98ft)

.32 Savage Model 1907

The .32 Savage Model 1907 was a fairly well-rounded gun, although it failed to be adopted by the US forces after it was overshadowed by the legendary Colt M1911 in military trials. After these trials, its manufacturers, the Savage Arms Corporation of Chicopee Falls, Massachusetts, needed a customer; in 1914, they found it in the Portugese armed forces, which had been severed from their German gun supplies. The Model 1907, and its successors in 1908 and 1915, were of a delayed-blowback action, the retardation created by the barrel turning through lugs before the slide could move backwards. The Savage was let down by it being possible for the firing pin actually to touch a round in the chamber – a hard knock could thus set it off – which necessitated the annoying unloading of the gun between firing.

SPECIFICATIONS

COUNTRY OF ORIGIN USA
CALIBRE .32 ACP
LENGTH 165mm (6.5in)
WEIGHT 0.63kg (1.37lb)
BARREL 95mm (3.75in), 6 grooves, rh
FEED/MAGAZINE CAPACITY 10-round detachable box magazine
OPERATION Delayed blowback
MUZZLE VELOCITY 244mps (800fps)
EFFECTIVE RANGE 30m (98ft)

Parabellum P'08 (Luger)

The Parabellum pistol's ancestry reaches back into the 19th century, but it is probably defined by the Pistole '08, known after its designer, Georg Luger. The transition from the 7.65mm calibre of Luger's early guns to 9mm Parabellum secured the popularity of the Pistole '08, and it was adopted by both the German navy and army. More than 2.5 million were subsequently produced between 1908 and 1945. Ironically, its visually distinctive toggle-lock mechanism was both a virtue and a problem – a virtue in that it worked well, but a problem in that it only worked well if kept clean, something far from easy in combat conditions. Nevertheless, it fired accurately (especially when fitted with an optional shoulder stock), was comfortable for the firer to hold and, even when simplified for wartime manufacture, exuded quality.

SPECIFICATIONS

COUNTRY OF ORIGIN Germany
CALIBRE 9mm Parabellum
LENGTH 233mm (8.75in)
WEIGHT 0.87kg (1.92lb)
BARREL 102mm (4in), 6 grooves, rh
FEED/MAGAZINE CAPACITY 8-round detachable box
OPERATION Short recoil
MUZZLE VELOCITY 380mps (1247fps)
EFFECTIVE RANGE 30m (98ft)

Bergmann-Bayard M1910

Not to be confused with the Mauser
C/96 which it superficially resembles,
the Bergmann-Bayard was developed by
Bergmann in the early 1900s, but mainly
manufactured by the Pieper company,
who purchased the rights from Bergmann
in 1908. The takeover was necessary, as
Bergmann had received an order for his
pistol from the Spanish Army which he
could not meet. Pieper also standardised
the weapon to 9mm, which had been
Bergmann's dominant choice, even though
he did experiment with other calibres
such as 10mm and .45in. The Bergmann-
Bayard was a heavy though solid weapon
with a short-recoil mechanism which was
essentially reliable. Apart from the Spanish
Army, Greek and Danish forces also
accepted the weapon as a standard side
arm, and it continued in service until the
end of World War II.

SPECIFICATIONS

COUNTRY OF ORIGIN Germany/Denmark
CALIBRE 9 x 23mm Bergmann-Bayard
LENGTH 254mm (10in)
WEIGHT 1.02kg (2.25lb)
BARREL 101mm (4in), 6 grooves, lh
FEED/MAGAZINE CAPACITY Short recoil
OPERATION 10-round detachable box magazine
MUZZLE VELOCITY 305mps (1000fps)
EFFECTIVE RANGE 30m (98ft)

Frommer Model 1910

Rudolf Frommer's Model 1910 was unusual for adopting a long-recoil principle of operation (where the barrel and bolt recoil for a distance greater than the entire length of the cartridge). The gun was actually developed some years earlier than its model date, but competition from the Roth-Steyr Model 1907 forced Frommer to improve the design before it could successfully enter the market. The principle was not ideal for a pistol, and though the Model 1910 was reliable enough, by 1930 Frommer was replacing it with a series of other handguns based on the Browning system of blowback operation (though not before another long-recoil pistol design, the Frommer 'Stop', was produced from 1912). Frommer's blowback guns proved to be simple, controllable firearms, and they became widely distributed throughout Europe.

SPECIFICATIONS

COUNTRY OF ORIGIN Hungary
CALIBRE 7.65mm Browning
LENGTH 184mm (7.25in)
WEIGHT 0.63kg (1.43lb)
BARREL 100mm (4in), 4 grooves, rh
FEED/MAGAZINE CAPACITY 7-round detachable box magazine
OPERATION Long recoil
MUZZLE VELOCITY 335mps (1099fps)
EFFECTIVE RANGE 20m (65ft)

Glisenti Model 1910

Designed by Revelli and initially manufactured in 7.65mm calibre by Siderurgica Glisenti until 1907, the Glisenti gun was developed further by Metallurgica Brescia gia Tempini, which responded to the Italian Army's request for a 9mm calibre weapon in 1910. The Modello 1910's fundamental problems centred on its construction. The left side of the gun was designed to come almost completely away for ease of cleaning, a feature which simply weakened the gun's endurance. Consequently, a less powerful cartridge, the 9mm Glisenti, was developed with the same dimensions as the more powerful Parabellum. Mixing up the two, as happened, could cause a breech explosion dangerous to the user. A further model of the Glisenti with minor safety changes emerged (Modello 1912), but as a combat gun it had severe limitations.

SPECIFICATIONS

COUNTRY OF ORIGIN Italy
CALIBRE 9mm Glisenti
LENGTH 207mm (8.15in)
WEIGHT 0.82kg (1.81lb)
BARREL 100mm (3.94in), 6 grooves, rh
FEED/MAGAZINE CAPACITY 7-round detachable box magazine
OPERATION Short recoil
MUZZLE VELOCITY 280mps (919fps)
EFFECTIVE RANGE 20m (66ft)

Colt M1911

Possibly the most famous and successful handgun of all time, the Colt M1911 and its variants stayed in service with US forces from 1911 to 1990, an incredible longevity. The Colt M1911 was born after a .38 automatic, designed by Browning, proved an ineffective man-stopper during service in the Philippines. Browning and Colt completely redesigned the gun in a powerful .45 calibre, and the US Army accepted it into service as 'U.S Pistol, Automatic, Caliber .45, Model 1911'. The M1911 and the M1911A1 (in production from 1926) achieved awesome success through their simplicity, reliability and power. The swinging-link short-recoil operation was rugged and the .45 round offered conclusive firepower. By the 1980s, the M1911A1 had become dated with its small magazine capacity and its difficulty in handling, and it was finally (and controversially) replaced by the Beretta 92.

SPECIFICATIONS
COUNTRY OF ORIGIN USA
CALIBRE .45 ACP
LENGTH 216mm (8.5in)
WEIGHT 1.13kg (2.49lb)
BARREL 127mm (5in), 6 grooves, rh
FEED/MAGAZINE CAPACITY 7-round detachable box magazine
OPERATION Short recoil
MUZZLE VELOCITY 253mps (830fps)
EFFECTIVE RANGE 35m (114ft)

Unceta Victoria

The Unceta Victoria was produced in Spain in the first decade of the 1900s, and offered a compact handgun in a relatively light 7.65mm calibre. As a company, Esperanza y Unceta was founded in 1908, and became a prolific gun manufacturer, though nowadays it is better known as the manufacturer Astra, which it became later, named after the Unceta logo. The Unceta Victoria was one of a (lengthy) line of European turn-of-the-century guns which paid a visible homage to Browning's ground-breaking handgun designs, and the general robustness of the Victoria imitation saw it achieve adoption by the French army as a sidearm. This, however, was to end when the Victoria was generally superseded by the Campo Giro, the latter gun going on to become the Spanish army's standard sidearm, with some examples seeing service in the Spanish Civil War.

SPECIFICATIONS

COUNTRY OF ORIGIN Spain
CALIBRE 7.65mm
LENGTH 146mm (5.75in)
WEIGHT 0.57kg (1.25lb)
BARREL 81mm (3.2in)
FEED/MAGAZINE CAPACITY 7-round detachable box magazine
OPERATION Blowback
MUZZLE VELOCITY 229mps (750fps)
EFFECTIVE RANGE 30m (98ft)

Mauser C/12

The Mauser C/12, or M1912, was the main military version of the famous 'broomhandle' C/96, which was designed by the three Feederle brothers and went into production with Mauser in 1896. Many variations followed, including models fitted with shoulder stocks, but the military model arrived in 1912 and is representative of most of the pistol series. Chambered for 7.63mm Mauser and, later in World War I, 9mm Parabellum, the C/96 was extremely well balanced despite its front-heavy appearance and was diligently machined. Its operation was a complex short-recoil and its integral magazine was top-loaded with chargers. This magazine was varied between 6-, 10- and 20-round versions, the latter proving impractical and soon being dropped. In short, the Mauser pistols were high-performance weapons but their downfall was their high cost of manufacture.

SPECIFICATIONS

COUNTRY OF ORIGIN Germany
CALIBRE 7.63mm Mauser or 9mm Parabellum
LENGTH 312mm (12.25in)
WEIGHT 1.25kg (2.75lb)
BARREL 139mm (5.5in), 4 or 6 grooves, rh
FEED/MAGAZINE CAPACITY 10-round integral box magazine
OPERATION Short recoil
MUZZLE VELOCITY 434mps (1425fps)
EFFECTIVE RANGE 60m (196ft)

Webley Self-Loading Pistol Mk 1

This unusual and heavy gun was an early foray by Webley & Scott into the world of the automatic pistol, although they themselves disliked this term and preferred 'self-loading'. A short-recoil weapon, the Webley Self-Loading Pistol Mk 1 used the immensely powerful .445 W&S Auto cartridge, for many years the world's most potent pistol round. This round was not transferable with the .445 ammunition used by Webley revolvers, a point which several unfortunates discovered when revolver cylinders exploded during firing the Auto cartridge. The Mk 1 was issued to the Royal Navy, the Royal Flying Corps, elements of the Royal Horse Artillery and some British police units, but it was never as popular with its users as the Webley revolvers. The force of the gun and its awkward angularity made it somewhat difficult to fire in rapid-response situations.

SPECIFICATIONS

COUNTRY OF ORIGIN UK
CALIBRE .445in W&S Auto
LENGTH 216mm (8.5in)
WEIGHT 0.62kg (1.37lb)
BARREL 127mm (5in), 6 grooves, rh
FEED/MAGAZINE CAPACITY 7-round detachable box magazine
OPERATION Short recoil
MUZZLE VELOCITY 228mps (750fps)
EFFECTIVE RANGE 30m (98ft)

Parabellum Artillery Model

The Parabellum Artillery Model (also known as the 'Long '08') was an early attempt to transform a standard pistol into a more potent carbine for use at longer ranges. In this case, it was simply achieved by extending the barrel of a standard '08 pistol to 190mm (7.5in), adding a leaf sight at the rear of the barrel, and supplying a wooden shoulder stock for attachment at the base of the pistol grip. In addition, the gun would also take the 32-round 'snail' magazine like that used by the Bergmann MP18, as well as the standard 8-round box magazine. More than 140,000 Artillery Models were made, the intention being to supply artillerymen, engineers and aircrew, who, it was thought, would need a greater range. However, overall the design lacked some plausibility and was never as popular in service as the standard pistol.

SPECIFICATIONS

COUNTRY OF ORIGIN Germany
CALIBRE 9mm Parabellum
LENGTH 311mm (12.4in)
WEIGHT 1.05kg (2.31lb)
BARREL 190mm (7.5in), 4 grooves, rh
FEED/MAGAZINE CAPACITY 8-round box magazine or 32-round snail magazine
OPERATION Short recoil
MUZZLE VELOCITY 380mps (1250fps)
EFFECTIVE RANGE 40m (131ft)

Webley & Scott Mk 6

The Mk VI was the last of a long line of redoutable Webley service revolvers produced from the late 1880s to the end of WWII. The Mk VI was officially in service between 1915 and 1945, and continued the Webley pistol's reputation for being heavy, accurate and reliable. It was also powerful. Firing the large .455 cartridge required a strong arm, but as a man-stopper it was undeniably successful and was used to great effect in close-quarters trench combat in WWI. A Pitcher/Greener revolver bayonet was also available, though not in popular use, as it made the gun even more unwieldy. One of the virtues of all Webley service revolvers was that they could be used under the filthiest of conditions without giving cause for concern, and their durability means that many collector's models are still being fired today.

SPECIFICATIONS
COUNTRY OF ORIGIN UK
CALIBRE .455 British Service
LENGTH 286mm (11.25in)
WEIGHT 1.09kg (2.4lb)
BARREL 152mm (6in), 7 grooves, rh
FEED/MAGAZINE CAPACITY 6-round cylinder
OPERATION Revolver
MUZZLE VELOCITY 200mps (655fps)
EFFECTIVE RANGE 30m (98ft)

Colt New Service Revolver M1917

After a period of using service revolvers of .38 calibre, the US Army turned once again to the potent .45 calibre round because of its combat experiences in the Philippines around the end of the 19th century. Finding that .38 rounds could often go straight through an assailant, rather than put him down, Colt brought out the .45 New Service Revolver (M1909) in 1909, which had greater stopping power. This was the last US service revolver to be adopted before the Colt M1911 automatic pistol took over the role, but the M1909 was improved in 1917 for wartime use as the M1917. The M1917 fired the rimless .45 ACP cartridge, as opposed to the rimmed .45 Colt of the M1909 (which was longer, but generated considerably less muzzle velocity), and loading such rounds into the gun could be speeded up by using three-round clips.

SPECIFICATIONS

COUNTRY OF ORIGIN USA
CALIBRE .45in ACP
LENGTH 273mm (10.75in)
WEIGHT 1.02kg (2.25lb)
BARREL 140mm (5.5in), 6 grooves, lh
FEED/MAGAZINE CAPACITY 6-round cylinder
OPERATION Revolver
MUZZLE VELOCITY 282mps (925fps)
EFFECTIVE RANGE 35m (115ft)

Colt Army Model 1917

Like the Smith & Wesson Model 1917, the Colt Model 1917 was one of the pistols purchased by the US Army which were converted to take the rimless .45in ACP cartridge and used to plug the military pistol shortages which had developed at the time due to the USA entering World War I. Again, like the Smith & Wesson, the new round necessitated the shortening of the cylinder and loading using three-round clips which enabled the rimless rounds to be ejected after firing. Prior to its conversion, the M1917 had been the Colt New Service Revolver, which began its life in 1897 and ranged across 18 different calibres. When standardised, some 150,000 M1917s were purchased by the US Army and some also crossed the Atlantic to the British Army in .445 calibre. The M1917's service outlasted World War I and continued until the end of the next world war.

SPECIFICATIONS
COUNTRY OF ORIGIN USA
CALIBRE .45in ACP
LENGTH 272mm (10.75in)
WEIGHT 1.14kg (2.51lb)
BARREL 140mm (5.5in), 6 grooves, lh
FEED/MAGAZINE CAPACITY 6-round cylinder
OPERATION Revolver
MUZZLE VELOCITY 265mps (870fps)
EFFECTIVE RANGE 30m (98ft)

S&W 'Hand Ejector' Model 1917

The Model 1917 was part of a US action to remedy a shortage of front-line pistols among US Army troops on the Western Front during World War I. As the standard service revolver at the time (Colt M1911 automatic) was .45 ACP calibre, the US forces purchased more than 150,000 Smith & Wesson revolvers and converted them to fire that round. This weapon thus become known as the M1917. Being a rimless round, the .45 ACP had to be loaded into the revolver in special three-round clips, otherwise the ejectors had no edge on which to gain purchase for cartridge removal. This situation was remedied on the commercial market in the 1920s by the Peters Cartridge Company, which developed a .45 rimmed round called the '.45 Auto Rim'. The M1917 was a good, solid revolver which gave service well beyond the end of the war in 1918.

SPECIFICATIONS

COUNTRY OF ORIGIN USA
CALIBRE .45in ACP
LENGTH 274mm (10.80in)
WEIGHT 1.02kg (2.25lb)
BARREL 140mm (5.5in), 6 grooves, lh
FEED/MAGAZINE CAPACITY 6-round cylinder
OPERATION Revolver
MUZZLE VELOCITY 265mps (870fps)
EFFECTIVE RANGE 40m (132ft)

Steyr Model 1917

The Steyr M1917 was a later variation of the estimable Steyr M1912 pistol, one of the finest handguns of the first half of the 20th century. The M1912 was the standard Imperial Austro-Hungarian (later Austrian) service pistol between 1912 and 1945, and, in common with other Austrian weapons, was also used by German forces during World War II (although in the latter case the gun was recalibrated for the ubiquitous German 9mm Parabellum round, rather than the more powerful 9mm Steyr). Known as the 'Steyr-Hahn' ('Steyr-Hammer') because of its external hammer, the M1912 had a rotating barrel for breech locking, the barrel turning 20° on firing before the slide disengaged and completed its recoil. Loading the Steyr's integral magazine consisted of inserting a charger of bullets down into the pistol's fixed magazine.

SPECIFICATIONS

COUNTRY OF ORIGIN Austria
CALIBRE 9mm Steyr or 9mm Parabellum
LENGTH 216mm (8.5in)
WEIGHT 0.99kg (2.19lb)
BARREL 128mm (5in), 4 grooves, rh
FEED/MAGAZINE CAPACITY 8-round integral box magazine
OPERATION Short recoil
MUZZLE VELOCITY 335mps (1100fps)
EFFECTIVE RANGE 30m (98ft)

Enfield .38

The Enfield pistol emerged from the demand for a less powerful British handgun that could be more easily handled by troops than the muscular .455 Webley pistols which served the British forces in WWI. A .38in 200-grain round was selected as appropriate for the role and the Royal Small Arms factory put their 'Pistol, Revolver, Number 2 Mark 1' into production in 1926/27. In most senses it was a copy of the Webley Mark VI, with modifications to the trigger and safety mechanisms. It was a double-action revolver, and this became the only method of operation when the Mark 1* was brought out with the hammer spur removed. Several different versions of the Enfield pistol were produced and it, along with the Webley Mk IV, became the standard issue service pistols for the British Army during WWII. Although efficient, they were not as prized as their German counterparts.

SPECIFICATIONS

COUNTRY OF ORIGIN UK
CALIBRE .38 British Service
LENGTH 260mm (10.25in)
WEIGHT 0.78kg (1.72lb)
BARREL 127mm (5in), 7 grooves, rh
FEED/MAGAZINE CAPACITY 6-round cylinder
OPERATION Revolver
MUZZLE VELOCITY 198mps (650fps)
EFFECTIVE RANGE 30m (98ft)

Astra Model 400

The Astra Model 400, also known as the Astra Model 21, was based on an earlier Spanish weapon, the 9mm Campo-Giro Model 1913, and retains the CampoGiro's distinctive 'air pistol' shape. The Astra entered production in the early 1920s and went on to enjoy a long service life into the 1950s with the Spanish and French armies, and with commercial interests worldwide. In terms of action, there is little exceptional about the Astra – it is a conventional blowback weapon. Its distinction comes from its ability to chamber and fire most 9mm rounds available on the market – even the .38 Colt Auto bullet. Rare versions were also made for 7.65mm ACP and 7.63mm Mauser ammunition. This versatility means that Astra Model 400s still crop up today, although worn pistols lose their ability to fire many modern 9mm rounds safely.

SPECIFICATIONS

COUNTRY OF ORIGIN Spain
CALIBRE 9 x 23mm Largo; 7.65mm ACP; 7.63mm Mauser
LENGTH 235mm (9.25in)
WEIGHT 1.08kg (2.38lb)
BARREL 140mm (5.5in), 6 grooves, rh
FEED/MAGAZINE CAPACITY 8-round detachable box magazine
OPERATION Blowback
MUZZLE VELOCITY 345mps (1132fps)
EFFECTIVE RANGE 40m (131ft)

Nambu 14th Year

The Nambu 14 was in many regards the same design as the disappointing Nambu 1904 handgun, but was cheaper to manufacture. It entered the Japanese market in 1925 and was officially accepted by the Imperial Japanese Army in 1927. The main difference from the Nambu 1904 was a safety catch on the receiver and, in 1939, the trigger guard's dimensions were expanded to enable the gun to be fired with a gloved hand. These changes did not, however, make the gun a dependable combat tool for those unfortunate enough to be equipped with it. The Nambu 14's magazine retaining spring and two recoil springs were prone to failure in corrosive climates – the pressure they imparted could make it difficult for a soldier to reload his weapon with sweaty or wet hands, thus making the Nambu 14 a dangerous weapon on which to rely.

SPECIFICATIONS
COUNTRY OF ORIGIN Japan
CALIBRE 8mm Nambu
LENGTH 227mm (8.93in)
WEIGHT 0.9kg (1.98lb)
BARREL 121mm (4.76in), 6 grooves, rh
FEED/MAGAZINE CAPACITY 8-round detachable box magazine
OPERATION Short recoil
MUZZLE VELOCITY 335mps (1100fps)
EFFECTIVE RANGE 30m (98ft)

Colt Detective Special

The legendary Colt Detective Special was in effect a Police Positive revolver rendered in a shorter 50mm (2in) barrel for the ultimate in portability and concealable convenience. The short barrel meant that the gun could be drawn quickly from a holster. It was also an especially light weapon, weighing in at only 0.6kg (1.3lb). Despite the extremely short barrel length, the gun remained businesslike in terms of power, owing to the .38 Special cartridge it fired. Although production of the Detective Special began in 1926, the gun was still going strong in the 1950s; yet, by then, a plethora of Colt variations were emerging. The standard Detective Special thus became the Model D.1 to distinguish it from other weapons. One feature which can be seen on some Detective Specials is a detachable hammer shroud which could be both self- and factory-fitted.

SPECIFICATIONS
COUNTRY OF ORIGIN USA
CALIBRE .38 Special
LENGTH 171mm (6.7in)
WEIGHT 0.06kg (1.31lb)
BARREL 54mm (2.13in), 6 grooves, rh
FEED/MAGAZINE CAPACITY 6-round cylinder
OPERATION Revolver
MUZZLE VELOCITY 213mps (700fps)
EFFECTIVE RANGE 30m (98ft)

Walther PPK

Although made famous by being the standard firearm of the fictional James Bond in Ian Fleming's books, the Walther PPK, although small, is a fairly unexceptional firearm. It emerged in 1931 as a smaller version of the PP pistol design for police use. As a double-action blowback weapon, it was reliable and light, although its varied calibres (.22 LR; 6.35mm Browning; 7.65mm Browning; 9mm Short) are somewhat indecisive when it comes to putting an opponent down. As a police weapon, the PPK has become dated, especially in its limited magazine capacity of only seven rounds, compared to the 15 available in a Beretta Model 92 or a SIG-Sauer P-225. However, its ease of portability and reliability mean that it will remain in service for many years to come amongst police and security units, who appreciate the ease with which it can be concealed.

SPECIFICATIONS

COUNTRY OF ORIGIN Germany
CALIBRE .22 LR; 6.35mm or 7.65mm Browning (.32 ACP); 9mm Short
LENGTH 148mm (5.8in)
WEIGHT 0.59kg (1.3lb)
BARREL 80mm (3.15in), 6 grooves, rh
FEED/MAGAZINE CAPACITY 7-round detachable box magazine
OPERATION Blowback
MUZZLE VELOCITY 290mps (950fps)
EFFECTIVE RANGE 30m (98ft)

Tula-Tokarev TT-33

The Tula-Tokarev 33 (TT-33) began in the late 1920s as the TT-30, an automatic pistol designed by Feodor Tokarev and based on the US M1911's swinging-link locking system. Tokarev simplified its components for the rigours of Soviet service, which involved machining the magazine feed lips onto the receiver itself, making the hammer and lock system in a detachable module at the back (more convenient for both manufacture and repair) and taking away the safety devices. The TT-33 became the Tokarev's dominant form from 1933. This differed from the TT-30 by having locking logs sited all around the barrel instead of just on top, something that speeded up production as barrel and locking lugs could be done at the same time. The TT-33 is still manufactured under licence today, in countries such as Poland and North Korea.

SPECIFICATIONS

COUNTRY OF ORIGIN USSR/Russia
CALIBRE 7.62mm Soviet
LENGTH 193mm (7.68in)
WEIGHT 0.83kg (1.83lb)
BARREL 116mm (4.57in), 4 grooves, rh
FEED/MAGAZINE CAPACITY 8-round detachable box magazine
OPERATION Short recoil
MUZZLE VELOCITY 415mps (1362fps)
EFFECTIVE RANGE 30m (98ft)

Beretta Model 1934

The Modello 1934 was the standard Italian Army pistol between 1934 and 1945. It was actually part of a long evolution of Beretta automatic pistols, developing from the Modello 1915/19, although with an external hammer like the Modello 1931. If anything, the hammer was a flaw in the design, as it remained operable even when the safety was on and the trigger locked - meaning that users had to take care. Another irritant was that the slide snapped forwards when an empty magazine was taken out instead of waiting open to receive a fresh magazine; thus the operator had to carry out a lot of slide operation to reload. Despite these problems and the fact that the 9mm Short round did not carry quite enough power for combat use, it was a generally superb and reliable weapon which is much sought after by collectors today.

SPECIFICATIONS
COUNTRY OF ORIGIN Italy
CALIBRE 9mm Short
LENGTH 152mm (6in)
WEIGHT 0.66kg (1.46lb)
BARREL 94mm (3.7in), 6 grooves, rh
FEED/MAGAZINE CAPACITY 7-round detachable box magazine
OPERATION Blowback
MUZZLE VELOCITY 280mps (920fps)
EFFECTIVE RANGE 30m (98ft)

Browning High-Power

In many senses, the Browning High-Power laid the groundwork for the modern combat handgun. Designed in the 1920s by John M. Browning and produced at Fabrique Nationale d'Armes de Guerre (FN) in Belgium from 1935, the High-Power featured a 13-round capacity, double-row magazine (nearly twice the capacity of its main rival, the Colt M1911) and a different locking mechanism to the Colt, one which used a shaped cam to draw the barrel downwards to lock in a more linear fashion than the Colt's swinging link. The result was a reliable, accurate side arm which armed men from both sides during World War II and went on to serve in the armed forces of more than 50 countries to this day. Variations in the 1980s kept the High-Power relevant to the market and, even though the design is starting to date somewhat, it remains internationally popular.

SPECIFICATIONS

COUNTRY OF ORIGIN Belgium/USA
CALIBRE 9mm Parabellum
LENGTH 197mm (7.75in)
WEIGHT 0.99kg (2.19lb)
BARREL 118mm (4.65in), 4 grooves, rh
FEED/MAGAZINE CAPACITY 13-round detachable box magazine
OPERATION Short recoil
MUZZLE VELOCITY 335mps (1100fps)
EFFECTIVE RANGE 30m (98ft)

Browning Double-Action

The Browning Double-Action (DA) is an advancement on the Browning High-Power, the main improvement being an ambidextrous de-cocking lever in place of a safety catch. This allows the user to drop the hammer safely, even when a round has been loaded into the chamber. However, the double-action mechanism means that, although the gun is completely safe in this mode, simply pulling the trigger through will fire the round. Fabrique Nationale d'Armes de Guerre (FN) continued the ambidextrous features – the magazine release switch, usually fitted on the right side, can be reversed for left-handed use. Apart from these features and a resculpting of the contours of the grip for two-handed use, the DA remains the same basic handgun as the High-Power, and its quality has made it a worthy replacement for the older weapon.

SPECIFICATIONS

COUNTRY OF ORIGIN Belgium
CALIBRE 9mm Parabellum
LENGTH 200mm (7.87in)
WEIGHT 0.905kg (1.99lb)
BARREL 118mm (4.65in), 6 grooves, rh
FEED/MAGAZINE CAPACITY 14-round detachable box magazine
OPERATION Short recoil
MUZZLE VELOCITY 350mps (1148fps)
EFFECTIVE RANGE 30m (98ft)

Radom wz.35

The Radom wz.35 was designed in Poland in the 1930s in an attempt to create a standardised Polish army side arm. It saw service between 1936 and 1945, although for most of the war years it was produced under German occupation. This period saw the quality of the weapon reduced, as the Germans tried to speed up gun production for their own use. As its appearance suggests, the Radom was beholden to the Colt-Browning system. Of short-recoil operation, its substantial weight enabled it to handle the 9mm round comfortably and overall it was an excellent gun. Its one drawback was an inadequate safety system, as it had no safety mechanism (the switch on the left of the receiver is for use during stripping) apart from a grip safety, although it did have a system for lowering the hammer onto a loaded chamber without firing.

SPECIFICATIONS

COUNTRY OF ORIGIN Poland
CALIBRE 9mm Parabellum
LENGTH 197mm (7.76in)
WEIGHT 1.022kg (2.25lb)
BARREL 115mm (4.53in), 6 grooves, rh
FEED/MAGAZINE CAPACITY 8-round detachable box
OPERATION Short recoil
MUZZLE VELOCITY 350mps (1150fps)
EFFECTIVE RANGE 30m (98ft)

Walther P38

Part of Germany's armaments rationalisation and expansion in the 1930s was the request for a new service pistol to replace the Luger P'08. Walther set to the task, modifying its PP pistol and going through various formats until the 9mm 'HP' (Heeres Pistole) was accepted, this then being designated the Pistole 38, or P38. The qualities of the P38 would see it in service throughout the 1950s and into the present day (known after 1957 as the P1). Well made, attractively plated in matt black and very reliable, the P38 featured a safety indicator pin which showed whether there was a cartridge in the chamber or not, and it also had an advanced double-action lock, which enabled the operator to fire the weapon from a hammer-down position with just a single pull on the trigger. It stands as one of the 20th century's best handguns.

SPECIFICATIONS

COUNTRY OF ORIGIN Germany
CALIBRE 9mm Parabellum
LENGTH 213mm (8.38in)
WEIGHT 0.96kg (2.11lb)
BARREL 127mm (5in), 6 grooves, rh
FEED/MAGAZINE CAPACITY 8-round detachable box
OPERATION Short recoil
MUZZLE VELOCITY 350mps (1150fps)
EFFECTIVE RANGE 30m (98ft)

Mauser HSc

The Mauser HSc started its production life in 1937. Like the Walther PP, it offered a double-action weapon of 7.65mm calibre – this was quite progressive for the Mauser company at the time, which was working in competition with the advanced Walther designers. Certain features, however, did distinguish it from the Walther. Even more of the hammer was concealed in the slide, with just a tiny portion left for cocking, and the whole gun was of a very sleek and minimalist design. The safety system actually disengaged the firing pin from its track into a recess that took it out of alignment with the cartridge. Production of the HSc (the initials standing for 'Hammerless, Self-Loading, Model C') ceased in 1945, but resumed commercially again in 1964. In the mid-1980s, Mauser licensed the HSc to the Italian arms company Renato Gamba.

SPECIFICATIONS

COUNTRY OF ORIGIN Germany
CALIBRE 7.65mm Browning (.32 ACP)
LENGTH 152mm (6in)
WEIGHT 0.64kg (1.32lb)
BARREL 86mm (3.38in), 6 grooves, rh
FEED/MAGAZINE CAPACITY 8-round detachable box magazine
OPERATION Blowback
MUZZLE VELOCITY 290mps (960fps)
EFFECTIVE RANGE 30m (98ft)

Liberator

The word 'cheap' does not begin to describe the Liberator, also known as the .45 OSS after its primary buyer, the Office of Strategic Services. The intention behind this weapon was to mass produce a single-shot weapon which could be used by resistance forces during the last stages of World War II. The gun was made out of the simplest possible steel pressings and stampings, ejection had to be accomplished using a short stick, the breech block was hand operated, and it had no rifling. Yet this crudity meant production was awesome – one million in three months alone. The gun was supplied with 10 rounds of ammunition and a set of univerally understandable cartoon-style instructions. Having almost no accuracy, it was intended primarily as an assassination tool. How many accomplished this task we will never know.

SPECIFICATIONS

COUNTRY OF ORIGIN USA
CALIBRE .45 ACP
LENGTH 141mm (5.55in)
WEIGHT 0.45kg (1lb)
BARREL 101mm (3.97in), smooth bore
FEED/MAGAZINE CAPACITY 1 round inserted directly into chamber
OPERATION Single shot
MUZZLE VELOCITY 250mps (820fps)
EFFECTIVE RANGE 10m (32.8ft)

Welrod Silent Pistol

A number of innovative weapons were developed during World War II for use by covert operatives and resistance fighters. The elimination of a single political figure or key military officer could cause very significant disruption to the enemy in a region. However, unless the operative was willing to undertake a suicide mission, the assassination had to be covert. In order to give the assassin a chance to complete the mission and escape, a silent firearm was desirable. A gun provided a range of options not available with a knife or other hand weapon; the target could be shot through a window or other opening without the assassin having to come into physical contact.

The Welrod assassination pistol was developed for the British Special Operations Executive and had an integral silencer. The only safety device was a grip safety, and reloading was manual rather than semi-automatic. To chamber the next round, the cap at the rear of the

weapon was twisted and pulled back, then pushed home again. Stopping power was less important to an assassin than to a combat soldier; a target that did not die immediately but succumbed to blood loss was just as dead as one who dropped instantly, so small-calibre weapons were not a major drawback.

SPECIFICATIONS

COUNTRY OF ORIGIN United Kingdom
CALIBRE 7.65mm (.301in) (.32 ACP)
LENGTH 310mm (12in)
WEIGHT 1.090kg (2.4lb)
BARREL 95mm (less silencer)
FEED/MAGAZINE CAPACITY 8-round magazine
OPERATION Rotary bolt
MUZZLE VELOCITY Not known
EFFECTIVE RANGE 20m (65ft)

SIG P-210

SIG's reputation for excellence in pistol design and manufacture was taken to new levels with the production of the P-210 pistol by the Swiss manufacturer shortly after World War II. Looked at from every angle, the P-210 is a superb gun which, like the P-226 in the US Army pistol trials in the 1980s, fell short of its potential military sales through its high price. A studied glance at the pistol confirms one of its most distinctive features – the slide is situated inside the frame and runs on rails. This means that the pistol hold its accuracy extremely well and its short recoil mechanism is very robust and dependable. The SIG P-210 entered military service in Denmark and police service in West Germany, and was sold commercially across the world. The P-210 handgun is still in production today in various target and operational configurations.

SPECIFICATIONS

COUNTRY OF ORIGIN Switzerland
CALIBRE 9 x 19mm Parabellum
LENGTH 215mm (8.46in)
WEIGHT 0.9kg (1.98lb)
BARREL 120mm (4.7in), 6 grooves, rh
FEED/MAGAZINE CAPACITY 8-round detachable box magazine
OPERATION Short recoil
MUZZLE VELOCITY 335mps (1100fps)
EFFECTIVE RANGE 40m (131ft)

Lebel M1886

Although the M1886 first went into production in the late 1800s, its place in the history of 20th century small arms is confirmed by its being the standard French rifle of World War I. In effect, the rifle was not a new one, simply a 1874 Gras rifle updated for use with an eight-round tubular magazine which was fitted beneath the barrel. This, and the fact that the M1886 was the first rifle to use smokeless powder in conjunction with an 8mm bullet, made it a truly advanced weapon for its time. It was, however, a heavy gun to use – empty weight alone came to more than 4kg (8.8lb). Furthermore, magazine loading could be a long and awkward business (although single rounds could also be loaded directly into the chamber) and the bolt action was susceptible to dirt. Despite these flaws, the Lebel carried the French forces throughout World War I.

SPECIFICATIONS
COUNTRY OF ORIGIN France
CALIBRE 8 x 50R Lebel Mle 1886
LENGTH 1295mm (50.98in)
WEIGHT 4.28kg (9.44lb)
BARREL 800mm (31.5in), 4 grooves, lh
FEED/MAGAZINE CAPACITY 8-round under-barrel tube magazine
OPERATION Bolt action
MUZZLE VELOCITY 715mps (2346fps)
EFFECTIVE RANGE 1000m (3250ft)

Infantry Rifle Model 1889

One of Fabrique Nationale's earliest jobs was manufacturing an adaptation of the German Mauser rifle for the Belgian market. Mauser had just introduced the clip-loading method of magazine replenishment (in response to Mannlicher developments) and this was carried through to the Belgian weapon for the new 7.65 x 53mm cartridge specific to the Belgian gun. Several features separated the Belgian Mauser from its German equivalent. The bolt handle was set at the back of the receiver bridge and the barrel encased in a thin steel jacket, the intention being to detach it from the distortions of the wooden furniture. The gun was also cocked on the closing of the bolt, rather than the opening, although Mauser changed this configuration for subsequent guns, as it slowed the speed of bolt operation and thus the rate of fire.

SPECIFICATIONS
COUNTRY OF ORIGIN Belgium
CALIBRE 7.65 x 53mm Belgian Mauser
LENGTH 1295mm (50.98in)
WEIGHT 4.01kg (8.82lb)
BARREL 780mm (30.6in), 4 grooves, rh
FEED/MAGAZINE CAPACITY 5-round integral box magazine
OPERATION Bolt action
MUZZLE VELOCITY 610mps (2000fps)
EFFECTIVE RANGE 1000m (3250ft)

Mannlicher-Carcano 1891

The Mannlicher-Carcano rifle began its life in the 1890s in Italy and established a pattern of rifles that would equip many Italian soldiers throughout both world wars. Its name comes from a combination of that of Salvatore Carcano, the rifle's overall designer, and that of the Mannlicher weapons, although only the Mannlicher magazine type was actually adopted in the final gun which emerged at the end of the design process. The first Mannlicher-Carcano issue was the M1891. This was a 6.5mm weapon which used a Mauser bolt action and a six-round integral box magazine that was loaded by chargers. The M1891 was a solid enough gun which became the standard Italian army weapon during World War I; there is little remarkable about its design or its performance. It did, however, set the scene for an interesting series of carbine models.

SPECIFICATIONS

COUNTRY OF ORIGIN Italy
CALIBRE 6.5 x 52mm Mannlicher Carcano
LENGTH 1290mm (50.79in)
WEIGHT 3.8kg (8.38lb)
BARREL 780mm (30.6in), 4 grooves, rh
FEED/MAGAZINE CAPACITY 6-round integral box magazine
OPERATION Bolt action
MUZZLE VELOCITY 730mps (2400fps)
EFFECTIVE RANGE 1000m (3250ft) plus

Moschetto Modello 1891

Like many European rifles in the 1890s, the Mannlicher-Carcano guns were soon recognised to be in need of a shortened, carbine version for use by cavalry troops. This need produced the Moschetto Modello 1891 per Cavalleria, otherwise known as the 'Truppo Speciale' model. It retained the same operating features as the parent rifle, but the length was quite dramatically reduced to 920mm (36.2in). Other features included a fixed bayonet which could be folded back when not in use to lie just beneath the barrel. Although generally intended for cavalry use, it also became a popular rifle with many auxiliary units, such as artillerymen, engineers and signallers, whose work demanded that weapons had compact dimensions for storage. Yet the size advantage could not alleviate the problems created in combat by the M91 series' underpowered 6.5mm cartridge.

SPECIFICATIONS

COUNTRY OF ORIGIN Italy
CALIBRE 6.5 x 52mm Mannlicher Carcano
LENGTH 920mm (36.2in)
WEIGHT 3kg (6.62lb)
BARREL 610mm (24in)
FEED/MAGAZINE CAPACITY 6-round integral box magazine
OPERATION Bolt action
MUZZLE VELOCITY 700mps (2275fps)
EFFECTIVE RANGE 600m (1950ft)

Mosin-Nagant Rifle

The Mosin-Nagant Rifle was a mix of designs from the Belgian brothers Emil and Leon Nagant and the Tsarist Russian officer Sergei Mosin. It was produced as a new standard rifle for Russian infantry forces and was issued as the M1891. Like most Russian weapons throughout the century, the key property of the Mosin-Nagant was its durability under the worst conditions. This was somewhat surprising, as the rifle had some fairly complex design features. Foremost amongst these was the two-piece bolt action, which actually allowed the cartridge being fired to remain free from magazine spring pressure. Yet the gun worked well and it became the standard Russian and Soviet service rifle (although hopelessly under-produced to meet demand) and emerged in several carbine models (the World War II model was the M1891/30).

SPECIFICATIONS

COUNTRY OF ORIGIN USSR/Russia
CALIBRE 7.62 x 54R Mosin-Nagant
LENGTH 1304mm (51.25in)
WEIGHT 4.43kg (9.77lb)
BARREL 802mm (31.6in)
FEED/MAGAZINE CAPACITY 5-round integral box magazine
OPERATION Bolt action
MUZZLE VELOCITY 805mps (2650fps)
EFFECTIVE RANGE 1000m (3250ft)

Artillery Musketoon Mle 1892

The Mle 1892 was one of the more distinctive-looking rifles developed in the late 19th century by André Berthier. It was part of a series of carbines (labelled 'Musketoon') which used the Mannlicher system of loading via a charger of rounds pushed down through the bolt into an integral magazine. Until 1915 (after some hard lessons were learned in the early stages of World War I), the three-round clip was used, then a new rifle was brought out which used a five-round clip. The Mle 1892 was a short, stocky rifle with a bulbous stock just in front of the trigger for the magazine housing and a cleaning rod running down the forestock. The short barrel and 8mm Lebel round only gave it a range of about 500m (1625ft), but this was more than adequate for most combat roles – most contemporary cartridges were overpowerful for the role for which they were required.

SPECIFICATIONS

COUNTRY OF ORIGIN France
CALIBRE 8 x 50R Belgian Mauser
LENGTH 940mm (37in)
WEIGHT 3.1kg (6.8lb)
BARREL 445mm (17.5in), 4 grooves, lh
FEED/MAGAZINE CAPACITY 3-round integral box magazine, clip-loaded
OPERATION Bolt action
MUZZLE VELOCITY 610mps (2000fps)
EFFECTIVE RANGE 500m (1640ft)

Mauser Gewehr 98

The Mauser Gewehr 98 was in production from 1898–1918 and was the standard German rifle during World War I. It is the archetypal Mauser weapon, and the bolt action established a model which is followed to this day. The bolt action consisted of three locking lugs, the third being beneath the bolt and which dropped into a recess in the receiver for extra locking safety. The gun was charger-loaded with no visible magazine and it proved itself a solid, reliable and accurate rifle which served soldiers well. It was consistently well crafted, although there was some deterioration in quality as the war ground on. Like most of its contemporaries, it was much more powerful than it needed to be for the time. World War II saw the Gewehr 98 in action once more, although by then it was mostly being replaced by a shortened version, the KAR 98.

SPECIFICATIONS
COUNTRY OF ORIGIN Germany
CALIBRE 7.92mm Mauser M98
LENGTH 1255mm (49.4in)
WEIGHT 4.14kg (9.13lb)
BARREL 740mm (29.14in), 4 grooves, rh
FEED/MAGAZINE CAPACITY 5-round integral box magazine
OPERATION Bolt action
MUZZLE VELOCITY 870mps (2855fps)
EFFECTIVE RANGE 1000m (3250ft) plus

Springfield Model 1903

Despite taking the name of the Springfield arsenal in Illinois, the Model 1903 actually originated with Mauser, who were asked to develop a new US service rifle under licence in the USA to replace the Krag-Jorgeson rifle used by US Army servicemen since 1892. The gun was first produced around the flat-ended .30 M1903 cartridge, then around the pointed M1906 (same calibre). From 1903, however, it was in production at Springfield and would stay in production until 1965. The reasons for its longevity were simple. With dimensions between full rifle and carbine, it was convenient to carry; it was accurate enough for sniper use; it rarely failed; and it was comfortable to use. A run of variations followed the original model (which can be distinguished by its straight stock, rather than pistol grip), including the M1903A4 sniper gun used in Vietnam.

SPECIFICATIONS
COUNTRY OF ORIGIN USA
CALIBRE .30in M1906
LENGTH 1097mm (43.19in)
WEIGHT 3.94kg (8.68lb)
BARREL 610mm (24in), 4 grooves, rh
FEED/MAGAZINE CAPACITY 5-round internal box magazine
OPERATION Bolt action
MUZZLE VELOCITY 853mps (2800fps)
EFFECTIVE RANGE 1000m (3250ft) plus

Arisaka 38th Year rifle

The Arisaka 38th Year Rifle took its
name from its designer, Colonel
Arisaka, and the year of the Japanese
Emperor's reign. It became the standard
Japanese infantry rifle between 1907 and
1944, and comprised a mix of Mauser and
Mannlicher features which had already
produced the 30th Year Rifle in the late
1890s. In many ways, the 38th Year
was a success because it was built with
the Japanese frame in mind. Its 6.5mm
cartridge was low-powered enough to be
controlled by a smaller figure, while the
pronounced length of the rifle gave some
advantage in bayonet clashes against
longer-limbed Caucasian opponents. A
sound enough weapon, the 38th Year
Rifle gave good service until the last years
of World War II, when shortages of raw
materials resulted in poorly constructed
and sometimes dangerously unstable
weapons.

SPECIFICATIONS

COUNTRY OF ORIGIN Japan
CALIBRE 6.5mm Japanese Service
LENGTH 1275mm (50.25in)
WEIGHT 4.31kg (9.5lb)
BARREL 798mm (31.45in), 6 grooves, rh
FEED/MAGAZINE CAPACITY 5-round internal box
magazine
OPERATION Bolt action
MUZZLE VELOCITY 730mps (2400fps)
EFFECTIVE RANGE 1000m (3250ft) plus

Lee-Enfield Mk II (SMLE)

The Lee-Enfield rifles are some of the best designed bolt-action rifles in history. They actually emerged out of a fusion between the smooth bolt operation of the earlier Lee-Metford rifles (so called after the designers James Paris Lee and William Metford) with a rifling developed at the Royal Small Arms Factory, Enfield Lock, in response to the arrival of cordite as the new cartridge propellant, which reduced the amount of fouling in the barrel. The first gun produced was the Lee-Enfield Mk I, issued from 1895, which had the new rifling and altered sights, and saw service in South Africa. In 1903, there arrived the Short Magazine Lee-Enfield Mk I. This began the true 'SMLE' configuration which would become the standard British infantry rifle format for many years to come. It had some 125mm (5in) removed from its barrel to reduce its length. The Mk II was not radically different from the Mk I, except

SPECIFICATIONS
COUNTRY OF ORIGIN UK
CALIBRE .303in British Service
LENGTH 1132mm (44.57in)
WEIGHT 3.71kg (8.18lb)
BARREL 640mm (25.19in), 5 grooves, lh
FEED/MAGAZINE CAPACITY 10-round detachable box magazine
OPERATION Bolt action
MUZZLE VELOCITY 617mps (2025fps)
EFFECTIVE RANGE 1000m (3250ft) plus

that it had new sights and barrel (the latter being shorter and lighter) and could be loaded by chargers.

Lebel-Berthier 1907/15

During the late 1800s, the French military authorities commissioned a new rifle to be designed in response to German and Austro-Hungarian weapon improvements. The result was a long series of carbines which issued from a committee headed by the estimable André Berthier. The first weapon was the Mousqueton Berthier Mle 1890, followed by the Mle 1892. Both were short, portable weapons which used the same bolt-action system as the Lebel 1886, although a violent recoil and muzzle-flash detracted from their initial popularity with front-line troops. The Mle 1907/15 was actually produced as a replacement for the standard Lebel rifle and was a slightly modified Mle 1907 Senegal rifle (known as the 'Colonial' model). It even went on to contract manufacture in the USA under Remington Arms-Union Cartridge Company.

SPECIFICATIONS

COUNTRY OF ORIGIN France
CALIBRE 8 x 50R Lebel
LENGTH 1303mm (51.3in)
WEIGHT 3.79kg (8.35lb)
BARREL 798mm (31.42in), 4 grooves, lh
FEED/MAGAZINE CAPACITY 3-round integral box magazine
OPERATION Bolt action
MUZZLE VELOCITY 715mps (2345fps)
EFFECTIVE RANGE 1000m (3250ft)

Lee-Enfield Mk III (SMLE)

From its entry into service in 1907, the Short Magazine Lee-Enfield (SMLE) Mk III became one of the seminal small arms of the 20th century. Officially designated Rifle No. 1, Mk III, it used the bolt action developed by the US arms designer James Lee and was produced at the Royal Small Arms Factory at Enfield Lock, United Kingdom, hence its name. Its virtues were of supreme value to British and Commonwealth soldiers across both world wars: a smooth, fast bolt action which could give 15rpm in trained hands; its capacious magazine which held 10 rounds and single rounds which could be directly loaded even with a full magazine; a sighted range of around 1000m (3280ft); rugged enough to withstand combat duties. Such was the quality of this gun that some of the three million produced still crop up in combat across the world.

SPECIFICATIONS
COUNTRY OF ORIGIN UK
CALIBRE .303in British Service
LENGTH 1133mm (44.6in)
WEIGHT 3.93kg (8.65lb)
BARREL 640mm (25.2in), 5 grooves, lh
FEED/MAGAZINE CAPACITY 10-round detachable box magazine
OPERATION Bolt action
MUZZLE VELOCITY 670mps (2300fps)
EFFECTIVE RANGE 1000m (3250ft) plus

Enfield Rifle M1917

The aborted British development of the .303in British Enfield Rifle No. 2 was not to be wasted on the USA, who rechambered the weapon successfully for the .3006 rimless US Service cartridge in 1917. A shortage of rifles at the beginning of the US part of World War I was behind the redevelopment and more than two million of the M1917 were subsequently made in two years of production before the end of the war in November 1918. The British and US weapons were almost identical in every way. Indeed, when more than 100,000 M1917s were supplied to the British Home Guard during World War II, a red stripe had to be painted around the stock to stop soldiers accidentally loading the rifles with the rimmed .303 British Service round. The M1917 also served after World War I in the hands of commercial buyers in the USA.

SPECIFICATIONS
COUNTRY OF ORIGIN USA
CALIBRE .30-06 US Service
LENGTH 1174mm (46.25in)
WEIGHT 4.36kg (9.61lb)
BARREL 660mm (26in), 5 grooves, lh
FEED/MAGAZINE CAPACITY 5-round detachable box magazine
OPERATION Bolt action
MUZZLE VELOCITY 853mps (2800fps)
EFFECTIVE RANGE 1000m (3250ft) plus

Mauser Kar 98K

German experiments with a carbine began, like many other European nations, in the late 1890s. The first issue was the M1898, otherwise known as the Kar 98, which was produced between 1899 and 1903, after which it was revised into the M1904. This latter weapon became the standard German rifle of World War I and, in 1920, was labelled as the Kar 98a. This rifle was still felt to be too long for convenient infantry use and, by the beginning of World War II, it had been further shortened to produce the Karabiner 98k (Kar 98k). There was little to separate the 98k from its longer parent. Visually it could be distinguished by its recess in the forestock and a less exposed muzzle than the Kar 98. What really separated the 98k was its prevalence and it became the standard German rifle of World War II. Its Mauser bolt action had all the qualities of strength and ease of operation that made for a successful gun and it retained a good combat accuracy over fairly long ranges. Even though quality of materials deteriorated by the end of the war, the 11.5 million Kar 98ks made gave reliable service in various hands well past the war years.

SPECIFICATIONS

COUNTRY OF ORIGIN Germany
CALIBRE 7.92mm Mauser M98
LENGTH 1110mm (43.7in)
WEIGHT 3.9kg (8.6lb)
BARREL 600mm (23.62in), 4 grooves, rh
FEED/MAGAZINE CAPACITY 5-round integral box magazine
OPERATION Bolt action
MUZZLE VELOCITY 745mps (2444fps)
EFFECTIVE RANGE 1000m (3250ft) plus

MAS Mle 1936

During the interwar period, French munitions experts sought to develop a cartridge to replace the outdated rimmed 8mm Lebel round. The result was the rimless 7.5 x 54mm Mle 1929. The MAS Mle 1936 was one of the weapons designed to take this new cartridge and has the questionable honour of being the last bolt-action weapon to become a standard military service rifle. Despite a rather awkward appearance, the Mas Mle 1936 was a robust and sound weapon. The bolt action was especially short on account of locking taking place at the very end of the receiver, even though this did necessitate the bolt handle being angled sharply forwards for proximity to the operator's trigger hand. The rifle's production life numbered nearly 20 years (some were adapted for use with rifle grenades in the 1950s) and it also came in a folding butt version for airborne troops.

SPECIFICATIONS

COUNTRY OF ORIGIN France
CALIBRE 7.5mm Mle 1929
LENGTH 1020mm (40.16in)
WEIGHT 3.78kg (8.33lb)
BARREL 573mm (22.56in), 4 grooves, lh
FEED/MAGAZINE CAPACITY 5-round integral box magazine
OPERATION Bolt action
MUZZLE VELOCITY 823mps (2700fps)
EFFECTIVE RANGE 1000m (3250ft) plus

Lee-Enfield No. 4 Mk 1

The beginning of World War II saw the SMLE Mk III as the standard British Army rifle, yet, by 1940, the need for a new version more amenable to wartime production restraints became evident. The Lee-Enfield Rifle No. 4 Mk 1 was the result – a weapon that, along with the Sten submachine gun and Bren machine gun, became synonymous with British troops. Visually, the most obvious change was the muzzle; the flat muzzle nosecap was cut back about 5cm (2in), with the exposed barrel taking direct fitment of the foresight and the new spike bayonet that replaced the sword bayonet. The rear sights were also moved to above the end of the bolt. A Mk 1* with a simplified receiver followed shortly after the introduction of the Mk 1. Like the SMLE, the No. 4 rifle was reliable, durable and had searching accuracy. About four million went through production.

SPECIFICATIONS

COUNTRY OF ORIGIN UK
CALIBRE .303in British Service
LENGTH 1128mm (44.43in)
WEIGHT 4.11kg (9.06lb)
BARREL 640mm (25.2in), 5 grooves, lh
FEED/MAGAZINE CAPACITY 10-round detachable box magazine
OPERATION Bolt action
MUZZLE VELOCITY 751mps (2464fps)
EFFECTIVE RANGE 1000m (3250ft) plus

Lee-Enfield Rifle No. 5

Lee-Enfield's Rifle No. 5 was the least satisfying of its bolt-action guns. It was born out of the demand from 1943 for a more compact weapon for use in the British Army's jungle campaigns in the Far East. The length of the SMLE in the jungle proved awkward, and an adaptation of the trusty Lee Enfield seemed the best option. The No. 5 was basically a No. 4 Rifle with a shortened forestock and barrel, the former featuring a rubber shoulder protector and the latter having a large flash hider. Both were essential, as the .303 round gave huge blast and recoil when fired from the new barrel length, but both modifications were ultimately inadequate for controlling the cartridge's power. This, combined with a flaw in the gun's sighting which meant that zero would shift from one day to the next, led to the gun being abandoned in 1947.

SPECIFICATIONS
COUNTRY OF ORIGIN UK
CALIBRE .303in British Service
LENGTH 1000mm (39.37in)
WEIGHT 3.24kg (7.14lb)
BARREL 478mm (18.7in), 5 grooves, lh
FEED/MAGAZINE CAPACITY 10-round detachable box magazine
OPERATION Bolt action
MUZZLE VELOCITY 610mps (2000fps)
EFFECTIVE RANGE 1000m (3250ft)

De Lisle Carbine

Many silenced weapons have entered the market since the De Lisle's birth in World War II, but few have surpassed the sheer level of noise reduction it attained. Its exceptional suppressor eliminates the muzzle report almost entirely, the only noises left being the bolt operation and the striker hitting the cap. Using a .45 ACP round (its magazine was that of the Colt M1911A1 pistol), it was still able to hit a target up to 400m (1312ft) away both accurately and powerfully. The British Commandos were the De Lisle's original users during the war, but, in the postwar period, many other special forces units utilised it when the need for accurate, silent killing arose. Indeed, some companies were still producing the De Lisle to order in the 1980s. Its only potential drawback was the need to work the bolt between each shot, which could expose the firer through his or her movement.

SPECIFICATIONS

COUNTRY OF ORIGIN UK
CALIBRE .45 ACP
LENGTH 960mm (37.79in)
WEIGHT 3.7kg (8.15lb)
BARREL 210mm (8.26in), 4 grooves, lh
FEED/MAGAZINE CAPACITY 7-round detachable box magazine
OPERATION Bolt action
MUZZLE VELOCITY 260mps (853fps)
EFFECTIVE RANGE 400m (1312ft)

Browning Automatic Rifle (BAR)

The Browning Automatic Rifle, or BAR, was something of an oddity, as it was classed as a rifle, but was more of a light machine gun in its dimensions. It was developed by Browning in 1917 and used in World War I in 1918, after which it was fitted with a bipod and became the BAR M1918A1, then the slightly improved BAR M1918A2. The BAR was a gas-operated gun which, depending on model and sub-variations, could fire either full automatic at two rates, 350 or 550rpm, or single-shot and full automatic. Firing full auto from a magazine that only held 20 rounds was somewhat incongruous, but, despite this and its heavy weight, the BAR became immensely popular with US servicemen during World War II and it remained in active service until 1957. In combat during WWII the BAR was often seen with the bipod removed, to save weight.

SPECIFICATIONS

COUNTRY OF ORIGIN USA
CALIBRE .30in M1906
LENGTH 1219mm (48in)
WEIGHT 8.8kg (19.4lb)
BARREL 610mm (24in), 4 grooves, rh
FEED/MAGAZINE CAPACITY 20-round detachable box magazine
OPERATION Gas
MUZZLE VELOCITY 808mps (2650fps)
EFFECTIVE RANGE 800m (2600ft) plus
CYCLIC RATE OF FIRE 550 or 350rpm

M1 (Garand)

The M1 became almost a symbol of US force during World War II and is the first self-loading rifle to be ever adopted as a standard military firearm. Designed by John C. Garand, a French-Canadian by birth, and produced from 1936, its main virtues were its self-loading gas operation, its solidity and durability (though it was also heavy), and its manufacture in enormous numbers – up to six million by the time it ended production in 1959. The negatives of the M1 were that the eight-round clips had to be loaded full or not at all – single rounds could not be added to a clip from which rounds had already been fired – and a loud 'ping' when the magazine emptied its last round which could act as an advertisement of vulnerability to the enemy. (Cunning GIs would throw empty clips to simulate their running out of ammunition, tempting unwary enemy soldiers out of cover.)

SPECIFICATIONS
COUNTRY OF ORIGIN USA
CALIBRE US .30-06
LENGTH 1103mm (43.5in)
WEIGHT 4.37kg (9.5lb)
BARREL 610mm (24in), 4 grooves, rh
FEED/MAGAZINE CAPACITY 8-round internal box magazine
OPERATION Gas
MUZZLE VELOCITY 853mps (2800fps)
EFFECTIVE RANGE 500m (1650ft) plus

Nevertheless, these problems did not overshadow the greatness of the gun, which gave sterling service for the decades it was in service.

Simonov AVS-36

The Soviet Army's experience of automatic rifles began somewhat inauspiciously when, in the 1930s, they adopted the AVS-36 designed by Sergei Gavrilovich Simonov (although it is predated by Federov's Avtomat) without ensuring its performance through proper service trials. Like many later Soviet assault rifles, the gas piston was set above the barrel, yet its operation struggled to contain the power of the Soviet 7.62mm round and it was also susceptible to the ingress of dirt. These factors, combined with a hefty recoil and muzzle blast, curtailed the future of the AVS-36 and, by 1938, it was out of production, if not actually out of service. Its replacement was the Tokarev SVT, but Simonov did go on to design the quality SKS rifle which used the new M193 7.62mm intermediate round and saw service after the end of World War II.

SPECIFICATIONS

COUNTRY OF ORIGIN USSR/Russia
CALIBRE 7.62 x 52R
LENGTH 1260mm (49.6in)
WEIGHT 4.4kg (9.7lb)
BARREL 627mm (24.69in), 4 grooves, rh
FEED/MAGAZINE CAPACITY 15-round detachable box magazine
OPERATION Gas
MUZZLE VELOCITY 835mps (2740fps)
EFFECTIVE RANGE 500m (1640ft) plus
CYCLIC RATE OF FIRE 600rpm

Tokarev SVT-40

Feydor Vassilivich Tokarev not only produced a famous Soviet pistol (the TT-33), but also a fairly well designed gas-operated assault rifle, the Samozaryadnaya Vintovka obr 1938, or SVT-38. It was a lengthy gun with a simple locking action consisting of a block which was cammed downwards into a recess in the receiver floor, this being released by the backward motion of the bolt carrier. The SVT-38 had a heavy muzzle blast, but Tokarev controlled this through a six-baffle muzzle brake. The SVT-38 was superseded by the SVT-40 in 1940 and this became the dominant model, with some two million rolling off the production lines between 1939 and 1945. Visually, the two guns were very similar. The SVT-40 had its cleaning rod situated under the barrel, rather than against the side of the forestock. The SVT40's muzzle brake also came in six- or two-baffle versions. Everything else stayed almost exactly

the same. Variants of the SVT-40 were the AVT-40, which was modified to be capable of automatic fire, and the SVT-40, a carbine version.

SPECIFICATIONS
COUNTRY OF ORIGIN USSR/Russia
CALIBRE 7.62 x 52R
LENGTH 1226mm (48.27in)
WEIGHT 3.90kg (8.6lb)
BARREL 610mm (25in), 4 grooves, rh
FEED/MAGAZINE CAPACITY 10-round detachable box magazine
OPERATION Gas
MUZZLE VELOCITY 840mps (2755fps)
EFFECTIVE RANGE 500m (1640ft) plus
CYCLIC RATE OF FIRE Semi-automatic

Fallschirmjägergewehr 42

The 7.92mm Fallschirmjägergewehr 42 (FG 42) was developed specifically for the German parachute regiments at the request of the Luftwaffe, which was competing with the Wehrmacht in the early 1940s to produce an automatic rifle for its troops. Rheinmetall subsequently produced the FG 42, which was an innovative and professional weapon. Distinctive features included a gas-operated mechanism, a 20-round side-mounted magazine and a large plastic stock (later, as the war progressed, made of wood because of production problems). Capable of both semi-and full-automatic fire (at 750rpm), it could be used as an assault rifle and as a light infantry support machine gun, the latter function made possible by a permanently fitted bipod near the muzzle. Its in-line stock made it a precursor of many modern assault rifles.

SPECIFICATIONS

COUNTRY OF ORIGIN Germany
CALIBRE 7.92mm Mauser
LENGTH 940mm (37in)
WEIGHT 4.53kg (9.99lb)
BARREL 502mm (19.76in), 4 grooves, rh
FEED/MAGAZINE CAPACITY
20-round detachable box magazine
OPERATION Gas
MUZZLE VELOCITY 761mps (2500fps)
EFFECTIVE RANGE 400m (1312ft) plus
CYCLIC RATE OF FIRE 750rpm

M1 Carbine

The M1 Carbine has endured in popularity from its initial production date in 1942 until the present day. It was originally designed by Winchester as a light, portable weapon for second-echelon troops such as drivers and support personnel, but these very qualities led many frontline combatants to adopt the weapon. The M1's distinctive gas-operation system worked through gas pressure pushing back a short-stroke piston, which in turn drove back the operating rod which cycled the bolt. It worked well and the M1 became a popular gun, although its pistol cartridge made it only suitable for relatively close-range fighting. Important variants included the M1A1, which had a folding steel butt, and the M2, which could fire full automatic, and in total more than six million M1 or variants were produced during World War II.

SPECIFICATIONS

COUNTRY OF ORIGIN USA
CALIBRE .30in Carbine
LENGTH 905mm (35.7in)
WEIGHT 2.5kg (5.47lb)
BARREL 457mm (18in), 4 grooves, rh
FEED/MAGAZINE CAPACITY 15- or 30-round detachable box magazine
OPERATION Gas
MUZZLE VELOCITY 595mps (1950fps)
EFFECTIVE RANGE c.300m (984ft)
CYCLIC RATE OF FIRE M2/M3: 750rpm

MP 43/Sturmgewehr 44

The MP43 in every sense marked the genesis of the modern assault rifle. Gas operated, it fired the short and fairly low-powered 7.92 x 33mm Kurz cartridge which was deemed perfectly adequate for the 400m (1312ft) ranges typical of actual combat and enabled the gun to be a stable platform for full-automatic fire. Ironically, Hitler originally prohibited the gun's development when it was known as the Maschinenkarabiner 42 (H), so its name was changed to the MP43 to mask its continuance from Hitler. Once it had proved itself on the Russian Front and Hitler finally gave his blessing, it became known as the Sturmgewehr 44 (illustrated above). The impressive, controllable firepower afforded by the MP43/StG.44 impressed all sides during the war and, immediately after 1945, it became the inspiration for many of the modern assault rifles soldiers hold today.

SPECIFICATIONS

COUNTRY OF ORIGIN Germany
CALIBRE 7.92mm Kurz
LENGTH 940mm (37in)
WEIGHT 5.1kg (11.24lb)
BARREL 418mm (16.5in), 4 grooves, rh
FEED/MAGAZINE CAPACITY 30-round detachable box magazine
OPERATION Gas
MUZZLE VELOCITY 700mps (2300fps)
EFFECTIVE RANGE c.300m (984ft)
CYCLIC RATE OF FIRE 500rpm

Simonov SKS

Simonov's SKS carbine was a Soviet attempt to find a weapon suitable for firing the 7.62mm Short (Kurz) cartridge discovered in captured German automatic MP44s. Of course, in later years the AK-47 became the defining Soviet weapon for the intermediate round, but the SKS came first, being trialled in 1944 and produced from 1946. A simple, robust, if rather heavy, weapon, the SKS was a solid gun which, although soon relegated to ceremonial use within the Soviet Union, spread around the world through other communist armies within Europe and Asia. As a single-shot weapon, it could put out fire to about 400m (1312ft), an especially useful combat range. Although features such as the folding bayonet under the muzzle now appear anachronistic to the modern eye, the SKS will no doubt keep making appearances for many years to come.

SPECIFICATIONS

COUNTRY OF ORIGIN USSR/Russia
CALIBRE 7.62mm Soviet M1943
LENGTH 1022mm (40.2in) stock extended
WEIGHT 3.86kg (8.51lb)
BARREL 520mm (20.47in), 4 grooves, rh
FEED/MAGAZINE CAPACITY 10-round detachable box magazine
OPERATION Gas
MUZZLE VELOCITY 735mps (2410fps)
EFFECTIVE RANGE 500m (1312ft)
CYCLIC RATE OF FIRE Single shot

Kalashnikov AK-47

The AK firearms are the most produced and distributed series of small arms in history. The series started with the AK-47, developed just after World War II to provide an intermediate-range infantry weapon which was resilient and fast-firing. Part of Mikhail Kalashnikov's inspiration was the German MP44 and its use of the new 7.92mm Kurz cartridge. Although Simonov produced a weapon to the new specification which went into production before the AK-47, it was the latter that met with incredible success. The AK-47 was a simple gas-operated design using a rotating bolt. It had a chromium-plated barrel and generally high-quality machining and finishing. It took until 1959 to perfect the design and production processes, but once this had been achieved, the Soviets were left with a truly seminal firearm. It could operate under the harshest of conditions without malfunction, was easily maintained and could compete with any Western firearm. It was also capable of extremely swift production and the AK-47 spread around the globe.

SPECIFICATIONS

COUNTRY OF ORIGIN USSR/Russia
CALIBRE 7.62mm Soviet M1943
LENGTH 880mm (34.65in)
WEIGHT 4.3kg (9.48lb)
BARREL 415mm (16.34in), 4 grooves, rh
FEED/MAGAZINE CAPACITY 30-round detachable box
magazine

OPERATION Gas
MUZZLE VELOCITY 600mps (2350fps)
EFFECTIVE RANGE 400m (1312ft)
CYCLIC RATE OF FIRE 600rpm

MAS 49/56

The MAS 49 was France's attempt, in 1949, to give its infantry a self-loading rifle. Apart from the drawback of its unorthodox 7.5mm French Service round (only a small number were produced in 7.62mm NATO), the rifle was distinguished by its almost unfailing reliability due to solid manufacture (even if this did make it a little heavy for the infantryman to carry). It was externally reminiscent of the earlier MAS 39 rifle, but it worked through a gas-operation system in which the bolt was driven back directly by the gas blast, rather than through the use of a piston. The MAS 49 was followed into service by the MAS 49/56. This differed from the original weapon in that, whereas the original's muzzle was designed to accept hollow-tailed rifle grenades, the 49/56 had a flared grenade-launcher/muzzle brake and more exposed barrel.

SPECIFICATIONS

COUNTRY OF ORIGIN France
CALIBRE 7.5mm French Service
LENGTH 1010mm (39.76in)
WEIGHT 3.9kg (8.60lb)
BARREL 521mm (20.51in), 4 grooves, rh
FEED/MAGAZINE CAPACITY 10-round detachable box magazine
OPERATION Gas
MUZZLE VELOCITY 817mps (2680fps)
EFFECTIVE RANGE 500m (1312ft)
CYCLIC RATE OF FIRE Semi-automatic

EM-2 Assault Rifle

The story of the EM-2 Assault Rifle is that of a gun truly ahead of its time. It was designed in the United Kingdom shortly after World War II, as a replacement for the over-powerful .303 Lee-Enfield rifle, and intended to be the new standard British infantryman's weapon. The EM-2 was revolutionary in that it fired a 7mm short-cased cartridge with magazine and bolt system behind the trigger group in what is now known as a 'bullpup' layout. The result was surprisingly good. It was an accurate (it fired from a closed bolt), durable weapon which became destined for British Army service as Rifle, Automatic, 7mm No. 9 Mk. 1.; however, the USA objected to both the cartridge size and power, and the 7.62mm round was accepted as the NATO standard. The EM-2 thus had to be dropped, although history has shown that the principles of the EM-2 would be followed by even its critics.

SPECIFICATIONS

COUNTRY OF ORIGIN UK
CALIBRE 7mm British
LENGTH 889mm (35in)
WEIGHT 3.41kg (7.52lb)
BARREL 623mm (24.5in), 4 grooves, rh
FEED/MAGAZINE CAPACITY 20-round detachable box magazine
OPERATION Gas
MUZZLE VELOCITY 771mps (2530fps)
EFFECTIVE RANGE 400m (1312ft) plus
CYCLIC RATE OF FIRE 600–650rpm

Villar Perosa M15

Arguably the first submachine gun despite its double barrel, the Vilar-Perosa was made as a support weapon for Alpine troops and infantry, and could be fired from the hip (suspended on straps), as well as from a bipod. Much about the weapon was advanced. Its blowback action was retarded by the breech block turning 90° following a spiral track in the receiver, the winding action imposing a slight delay on both recoil and return. However, this delay did not stop the Vilar-Perosa firing at 1200rpm, a phenomenal rate of fire which was due to a very light bolt and the top-mounted magazines, which fed the cartridges by both spring and gravity. The Vilar-Perosa served through both world wars and was a significant contribution to weapons technology.

SPECIFICATIONS
COUNTRY OF ORIGIN Italy
CALIBRE 9mm Glisenti
LENGTH 533mm (21in)
WEIGHT 6.25kg (14.37lb)
BARREL 318mm (12.5in), 6 grooves, rh
FEED/MAGAZINE CAPACITY
25-round box magazine
OPERATION Delayed blowback
MUZZLE VELOCITY 365mps (1200fps)
EFFECTIVE RANGE 120m (400ft)
CYCLIC RATE OF FIRE 1200rpm

Bergmann MP18

The Bergmann MP18, also known as the Bergmann Muskete, was actually developed by Hugo Schmeisser in 1916, and heralded the emergence of the blowback submachine gun. It was intended for raids and trench-clearing operations in World War I, a role in which it was briefly – and successfully – tested in 1918. Conditions of the Versailles Treaty kept the MP18 out of German military hands for much of the interwar period, but the weapon was permitted in police hands, and returned to military use after Hitler's rise to power and stayed in production until 1945. The MP18 inspired many new designs with its reliable, straightforward blowback system and 450rpm firepower, and was later developed by Schmeisser into the MP28 (which in turn inspired the British Lanchester). It could only fire on full automatic from an open bolt position. One of the MP18's most defining elements was the long 'snail' magazine also used for

SPECIFICATIONS

COUNTRY OF ORIGIN Germany
CALIBRE 9 x 19mm Parabellum
LENGTH 815mm (32.09in)
WEIGHT 4.19kg (9.25lb)
BARREL 196mm (7.75in), 6 grooves, rh
FEED/MAGAZINE CAPACITY 32-round 'snail' or 20- or 32-round detachable box magazine
OPERATION Blowback
MUZZLE VELOCITY 395mps (1295fps)
EFFECTIVE RANGE 70m (230ft)
CYCLIC RATE OF FIRE 450rpm

the Parabellum Long '08, although this was quickly phased out in favour of a stick magazine holding 20 rounds, which had always been Schmeisser's preferred design.

OVP

Although the Vilar-Perosa can justifiably lay claim to being the world's first submachine gun, its double-barrelled configuration marred its convenience of use. An attempt to create a more plausible weapon resulted in the 9mm OVP. This was one half of the Vilar-Perosa reconfigured in a standard rifle format with the addition of a wooden stock and trigger – although there was still no furniture forward of the trigger guard. Cocking also had to be redesigned and this was done on the OVP by pulling back a sleeve which wrapped around the receiver. A double-trigger unit gave the firer the option of automatic or single-shot fire. The OVP did not have a very long service life, but it was a step along the way to the very satisfying Beretta designs which would emerge following World War I.

SPECIFICATIONS
COUNTRY OF ORIGIN Italy
CALIBRE 9 x 19mm Glisenti
LENGTH 850mm (33.5in)
WEIGHT 3.26kg (7.19lb)
BARREL 305mm (12in), 6 grooves, rh
FEED/MAGAZINE CAPACITY 25-round detachable box magazine (top-mounted)
OPERATION Delayed blowback
MUZZLE VELOCITY 380mps (1247fps)
EFFECTIVE RANGE 120m (400ft)
CYCLIC RATE OF FIRE 900rpm

Thompson M1921

The Thompson submachine gun was designed by US Army officer Brigadier-General John Tagliaferro Thompson. In 1921, it entered the commercial market and immediately won respect. Firing the .45 ACP cartridge fed from box magazines or large-capacity drum magazines, it was a powerful weapon which fired at 800rpm with a Cutts Compensator at the muzzle to keep the gun under control. Its basic operation was delayed-blowback, the delay initially provided by the Blish Hesitation Lock, which consisted of two metal blocks which slid against each other at an oblique angle. It was actually unnecessary, and many later Thompsons did away with it. Both the US police and their criminal opponents took to the Thompson gun, and it was some years before its underworld image was overcome.

SPECIFICATIONS

COUNTRY OF ORIGIN USA
CALIBRE .45in M1911
LENGTH 857mm (33.75in)
WEIGHT 4.88kg (10.75lb)
BARREL 266mm (10.5in), 6 grooves, rh
FEED/MAGAZINE CAPACITY 18-, 20- or 30-round detachable box magazine; 50- or 100-round drum magazine
OPERATION Delayed blowback
MUZZLE VELOCITY 280mps (920fps)
EFFECTIVE RANGE 120m (400ft)
CYCLIC RATE OF FIRE 800rpm

Thompson M1928

The Thompson M1928 was perhaps the most well-known of the Thompson submachine gun series, though it actually differed little from the M1921 apart from having a reduced rate of fire and some variants came without the foregrip. The M1928 was the first Thompson to enter military service, with the US Marines, yet manufacture did not reach substantial levels until the beginning of WWII when France, Britain and Yugoslavia needed reliable small arms with high rates of fire. However the M1928 was a complex machined weapon with laborious production processes. Nevertheless,

it gave sterling service to many Allied troops and, admittedly, US criminal organisations. The M1 submachine gun was the Thompson M1928 redesigned for mass production by the Savage Arms Co. in 1942. The M1, a simple blowback design, also removed the M1928's barrel cooling fins and compensator. It went into widespread US Army use, but was itself superseded by the M1A1 which had a standard firing pin configuration rather than the hammer type used in the M1 and M1928. In this later form the Thompson lived on until the 1960s.

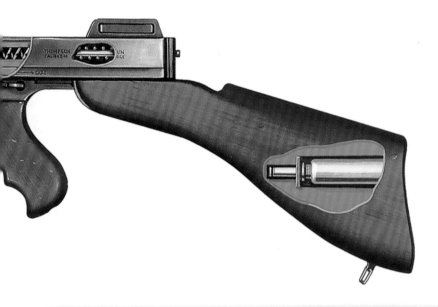

SPECIFICATIONS

COUNTRY OF ORIGIN USA
CALIBRE .45in M1911
LENGTH 857mm (33.75in)
WEIGHT 4.88kg (10.75lb)
BARREL 266mm (10.5in), 6 grooves, rh
FEED/MAGAZINE CAPACITY 18-, 20- or 30-round detachable box magazine; 50-or 100-round drum magazine

OPERATION Delayed blowback
MUZZLE VELOCITY 280mps (920fps)
EFFECTIVE RANGE 120m (393ft)
CYCLIC RATE OF FIRE 700rpm

Erma MPE

The most famous submachine guns to emerge from Erma were the landmark MP38 and MP40, but the MPE was an important step towards those designs. Designed by the talented Heinrich Vollmer, the MPE entered production in 1930, but the rights of manufacture were eventually sold on to Berthold Geipel GmbH in 1934, which took it to larger scale production – in this form it became known as the EMP (Erma Machinenpistole). The distinctive features of the MPE/EMP were its single-shot or full-auto selection facility, wooden foregrip, side-fed magazine and telescoping return-spring casing, the last a subsequent element of the MP38. Customers for the MPE included France, Mexico, Bolivia and Paraguay in the Gran Chaco War (1932–35), and various groups during the Spanish Civil War.

SPECIFICATIONS

COUNTRY OF ORIGIN Germany
CALIBRE 9mm Parabellum
LENGTH 902mm (35.5in)
WEIGHT 4.15kg (9.13lb)
BARREL 254mm (10in), 6 grooves, rh
FEED/MAGAZINE CAPACITY 20- or 32-round box magazine
OPERATION Blowback
MUZZLE VELOCITY 395mps (1300fps)
EFFECTIVE RANGE 70m (230ft)
CYCLIC RATE OF FIRE 500rpm

Suomi Model 31

The Suomi Model 31 was the product of Aimo Johannes Lahti, a designer for the Finnish State Arsenal. His first significant product, the 7.63/7.65mm M26, was not a great commercial success, unlike the M31, its successor. Typically for the 1930s, the M31 was a very well machined blowback-operated weapon which was judiciously made for the increasingly important 9mm Parabellum round. It could be loaded with with either 20- or 50-round box magazines or an influential 71-round drum, which was copied by Shpagin for the PPSh-41. The M31 ended its production in 1944, but stayed in use long after the war – although, in the 1950s, it was converted to use the Carl Gustav's 36-round box magazine. Clients for the M31 reached from Switzerland and Poland to South American countries.

SPECIFICATIONS

COUNTRY OF ORIGIN Finland
CALIBRE 9 x 19mm Parabellum
LENGTH 870mm (34.25in)
WEIGHT 4.87kg (10.74lb)
BARREL 318mm (12.52in), 6 grooves, rh
FEED/MAGAZINE CAPACITY 30- or 50-round detachable box magazine or 71-round drum
OPERATION Blowback
MUZZLE VELOCITY 400mps (1310fps)
EFFECTIVE RANGE 300m (984ft)
CYCLIC RATE OF FIRE 900rpm

PPD-34/38

In the PPD-34/38, we get a foretaste of the superb PPSh-41 in terms of layout and feed. Yet the PPD weapons were actually Degtyarev's amalgamation of three existing non-Soviet weapons: the Finnish Suomi m/1931 and the German MP18 and MP28. From the m/1931 came the 71-round drum magazine, but the PPD also came with a 25-round curved box. From the German weapons came most of the PPD's actual operating system, a simple blowback. As a result of the generally high (and ultimately too expensive) standard of production and parts that went into the PPD weapons, all those made between 1934 and 1940 were generally sound weapons. This quality was nothing but enhanced by the chromium plating of the barrel to resist wear, a feature which was carried forward into the PPSh-41.

SPECIFICATIONS

COUNTRY OF ORIGIN USSR/Russia
CALIBRE 7.62 x 25mm Soviet
LENGTH 780mm (30.71in)
WEIGHT 3.76kg (8.25lb)
BARREL 272mm (10.75in), 4 grooves, rh
FEED/MAGAZINE CAPACITY 25-round detachable box magazine or 71-round drum
OPERATION Blowback
MUZZLE VELOCITY 500mps (1640fps)
EFFECTIVE RANGE 100m (328ft) plus
CYCLIC RATE OF FIRE 800rpm

Star SI35

The Star SI35 was a strong foray into submachine gun design let down by its complexity of manufacture. It was developed by Bonifacio Echeverria in the 1930s as part of a series intended to give Spain its own submachine gun weaponry. It was a delayed blowback gun which had the ability to switch its rates of fire between 300rpm and 700rpm, though this could not easily be done in the heat of battle. Another unusual feature was that the bolt was held back and open once the magazine was empty, a feature more common in assault rifles. The SI35 was a sound weapon in principle and in operation, and it was trialled by Britain and the US during WWII. However, the complex engineering process it used meant that both countries rejected it for home-grown options.

SPECIFICATIONS

COUNTRY OF ORIGIN Spain
CALIBRE 9 x 23mm Largo
LENGTH 900mm (35.45in)
WEIGHT 3.74kg (8.25lb)
BARREL 269mm (10.6in), 6 grooves, rh
FEED/MAGAZINE CAPACITY 10-, 30- or 40-round detachable box magazine
OPERATION Delayed blowback
MUZZLE VELOCITY 410mps (1345fps)
EFFECTIVE RANGE 50m (164ft)
CYCLIC RATE OF FIRE 300 or 700rpm

Beretta Model 1938/42

In World War II all countries had to find a balance between quality and quantity in terms of submachine gun production. In Italy, Beretta more than succeeded in this balance by turning the excellent Beretta 1938A into a form more suited to heavy wartime manufacture. This was the Model 1938/42. It closely followed the 1938A, but simplification had removed the perforated barrel jacket and shortened the barrel slightly. In addition, the metal parts of the gun were more straightforwardly engineered from sheet steel. A dust cover was also fitted to the bolt handle to stop dust and sand intrusion (a modification made from experience in the Western desert). The Model 1938/42 would only accept standard 9mm Parabellum ammunition, but it still depended on Beretta-made magazines to feed effectively.

SPECIFICATIONS

COUNTRY OF ORIGIN Italy
CALIBRE 9mm Parabellum
LENGTH 798mm (31.4in)
WEIGHT 2.72kg (6lb)
BARREL 198mm (7.79in), 6 grooves, rh
FEED/MAGAZINE CAPACITY 34-round detachable box magazine
OPERATION Blowback
MUZZLE VELOCITY 395mps (1295fps)
EFFECTIVE RANGE 70m (230ft)
CYCLIC RATE OF FIRE 550rpm

MAS 38

Although the curved line between muzzle and stock gives the MAS 38 an awkward appearance, it was actually a fine weapon. Yet, as its 7.65mm French Long cartridge was only made in France, international sales were not forthcoming. The MAS 38 was a blowback weapon with an especially long bolt travel and a return spring that ran the length of the stock. Recoil was controlled by the low power of the round and the stock's alignment with the barrel, thus resisting muzzle climb. Useful features included a cocking handle that was separate from the bolt when firing and a hinged flap that closed over the magazine aperture when a magazine was withdrawn. The MAS 38 was in production between 1938 and 1949; postwar ammunition standardisation curtailed its future.

SPECIFICATIONS

COUNTRY OF ORIGIN France
CALIBRE 7.65mm French Long
LENGTH 734mm (28.9in)
WEIGHT 2.87kg (6.33lb)
BARREL 224mm (8.82in), 4 grooves, rh
FEED/MAGAZINE CAPACITY 32-round detachable box magazine
OPERATION Blowback
MUZZLE VELOCITY 351mps (1152fps)
EFFECTIVE RANGE 40m (131ft)
CYCLIC RATE OF FIRE 600rpm

MP38

The MP38 gave the German forces exactly what they needed for the blitzkrieg conditions of World War II – a light gun which could provide a high rate of fire and be manufactured in sufficient quantities to meet demand. Its production, which relied on economical metal stampings rather than expensive machining, enabled mass production on a new scale typical of Germany's greater mechanisation of war. Its actual operation was a straightforward blowback and the weapon gained a good reputation for reliability. However, the MP38 was also prone to accidental firing if knocked (as it fired from an open-bolt position) and a modified version, the MP38/40, was produced which used the cocking handle as a locking pin for the breech when not being fired.

SPECIFICATIONS

COUNTRY OF ORIGIN Germany
CALIBRE 9mm Parabellum
LENGTH 832mm (32.75in) stock extended; 630mm (24.75in) stock folded
WEIGHT 4.1kg (9.1lb)
BARREL 247mm (9.75in), 6 grooves, rh
FEED/MAGAZINE CAPACITY 32-round box magazine
OPERATION Blowback
MUZZLE VELOCITY 395mps (1300fps)
EFFECTIVE RANGE 70m (230ft)
CYCLIC RATE OF FIRE 500rpm

PPD-40

Following the PPD-34/38 came the last in the line of the PPD weapons – the PPD40. In terms of performance, the gun was identical to the PPD-34/38, giving the same rpm and the same muzzle velocity, with good reliability and resistance to dirt and mishandling. The PPD-40, however, steered away from the complex machining processes of its predecessor and was altogether an easier weapon to manufacture. It also accepted the magazine through a hole set into the forestock instead of snapping into a channel. Although production had been simplified, it still fell short of the rapid stamping and pressing techniques that were demanded under wartime exigencies and thus the entry of weapons such as the PPSh-41 pushed the PPD-40 out of production.

SPECIFICATIONS

COUNTRY OF ORIGIN USSR/Russia
CALIBRE 7.62 x 25mm Soviet
LENGTH 777mm (30.6in)
WEIGHT 3.7kg (8.16lb)
BARREL 269mm (10.6in), 4 grooves, rh
FEED/MAGAZINE CAPACITY 25-round detachable box magazine or 71-round drum
OPERATION Blowback
MUZZLE VELOCITY 500mps (1640fps)
EFFECTIVE RANGE 100m (328ft) plus
CYCLIC RATE OF FIRE 800rpm

MP40

Although the MP38 relied on rationalised methods of manufacture, its replacement, the MP40, took the process further and enabled more than one million to be produced during World War II. The MP40 relied even more on processes of steel pressing, spot welding and sub-assembly than its predecessor and thus submachine gun manufacture was able to keep pace with demand, even when the second front opened up with the Soviet Union in 1941. The emphasis on subassembly and simple manufacturing techniques meant that most small-scale engineering plants could produce the gun's various components. Both the MP38 and the MP40 are often referred to as the 'Schmeisser', but they were the products of Erma designer Heinrich Vollmer – Hugo Schmeisser was not involved at any stage.

SPECIFICATIONS

COUNTRY OF ORIGIN Germany
CALIBRE 9mm Parabellum
LENGTH 832mm (32.75in) stock extended; 630mm (24.75in) stock folded
WEIGHT 3.97kg (8.75lb)
BARREL 248mm (9.75in), 6 grooves, rh
FEED/MAGAZINE CAPACITY 32-round box magazine
OPERATION Blowback
MUZZLE VELOCITY 395mps (1300fps)
EFFECTIVE RANGE 70m (230ft)
CYCLIC RATE OF FIRE 500rpm

Fürrer MP41/44

The Fürrer MP41/44's awkward appearance hints at the impracticality and inefficiency of its internal workings. It was a rushed adoption by the Swiss Army in 1940, which needed a submachine gun for its forces. Not only was this after the army rejected a competent SIG weapon, but also the MP41/44 did not emerge until three years later because of production problems. Behind the MP41/44 was the figure of Colonel Fürrer of the Federal Arms Factory, a man obsessed with applying Maxim's toggle lock to all manner of weapons from submachine guns to artillery. The result in the MP41's case was an extraordinarily complex gun which was unreliable, manufactured in insufficient numbers and uncomfortable to use. Frustrated, the Swiss Army ended up turning to Hispano-Suiza for its SMGs.

SPECIFICATIONS

COUNTRY OF ORIGIN Switzerland
CALIBRE 9mm Parabellum
LENGTH 775mm (30.5in)
WEIGHT 5.2kg (11.5lb)
BARREL 247mm (9.72in), 6 grooves, rh
FEED/MAGAZINE CAPACITY 40-round detachable box magazine
OPERATION Recoil, toggle-locked
MUZZLE VELOCITY 395mps (1295fps)
EFFECTIVE RANGE 70m (230ft)
CYCLIC RATE OF FIRE 800rpm

Lanchester

The 9mm Lanchester was incredibly well crafted, expensive and a joy to use. It was designed for RAF and Royal Navy use (although only the Navy took receipt) after Dunkirk by George Lanchester of the Sterling Armament Company, and was almost entirely a copy of the German Bergmann MP28. Whereas the Bergmann used the furniture of the Mauser 98k, the Lanchester used that of the Short Magazine Lee-Enfield (SMLE), including the bayonet fitting. Other differences included the solid brass magazine housing, an indication of the incredible quality of materials and machining in everything from the stock to the breech-block mechanism. It fired extremely well and was loved by its owners, but its high cost and long production time meant that the crude Sten became the dominant British submachine gun.

SPECIFICATIONS

COUNTRY OF ORIGIN UK
CALIBRE 9mm Parabellum
LENGTH 850mm (33.5in)
WEIGHT 4.34kg (9.56lb)
BARREL 203mm (8in), 6 grooves, rh
FEED/MAGAZINE CAPACITY 50-round box magazine
OPERATION Blowback
MUZZLE VELOCITY 380mps (1247fps)
EFFECTIVE RANGE 70m (230ft)
CYCLIC RATE OF FIRE 600rpm

PPSh-41

The PPSh-41 was designed to meet the urgent need for submachine guns in the Soviet Union in the wake of the German invasion in 1941. Designed by Georgiy Shpagin, it had a simple blowback action and relied on processes of metal stamping for ease of production, although it also had a chromed barrel lining. More than five million were made by manufacturers ranging from industrial plants to village workshops. Loaded with either a 71-round drum or 35-round box magazine, it could fire at 900rpm with astonishing reliability. The PPSh-41 was robust, resistant to mishandling and dirt, and powerful, and therefore both Soviet and German soldiers were eager to get their hands on the weapon and it became almost a motif of Soviet resistance to the Nazi invasion. It equipped the many partisans who were such a thorn in the German's side, and would continue to function without any form of regular maintenance, although field stripping was

very straightforward, thanks to the hinged receiver. Following the war, it was used extensively by the North Koreans and other communist countries and still turns up in action today.

SPECIFICATIONS

COUNTRY OF ORIGIN USSR/Russia
CALIBRE 7.62mm M1930
LENGTH 838mm (33in) stock extended
WEIGHT 3.64kg (8lb)
BARREL 266mm (10.5in), 4 grooves, rh
FEED/MAGAZINE CAPACITY 35-round box or 71-round drum magazine
OPERATION Blowback
MUZZLE VELOCITY 490mps (1600fps)
EFFECTIVE RANGE 120m (400ft)
CYCLIC RATE OF FIRE 900rpm

Owen

Australia is one of the few nations to have experimented with top-mounted magazines on submachine guns – in the Owen, the experiment paid off. The Owen was adopted as a last-ditch measure in 1940, when the United Kingdom was unable to supply Australia with Sten guns. Despite its appearance, the Owen was comfortable to use and the vertical feed system worked efficiently and reliably, and it soon became popular with Australian frontline troops. The basic Owen came in two variants: early models had a solid frame and featured barrel-cooling fins; the later, more numerous model had a skeletal stock and the cooling fins were removed. Although heavy and featuring necessarily offset sights, the Owen had no serious defects and its use after the war continued into the 1960s.

SPECIFICATIONS

COUNTRY OF ORIGIN Australia
CALIBRE 9mm Parabellum
LENGTH 813mm (32in)
WEIGHT 4.21kg (9.28lb)
BARREL 247mm (9.75in), 7 grooves, rh
FEED/MAGAZINE CAPACITY 33-round detachable box magazine
OPERATION Blowback
MUZZLE VELOCITY 380mps (1247fps)
EFFECTIVE RANGE 70m (230ft)
CYCLIC RATE OF FIRE 700rpm

Reising Model 55

Developed just prior to World War II by the Harrington and Richardson Arms Co., the Reising Models 50 and 55 rejected the open-bolt blowback system of most submachine guns in favour of firing from a closed bolt, the firing pin being operated within the breech block by a complex system of levers. The M50's complexity proved its undoing. The ingress of dirt through the cocking-lever track under the fore-end could quickly stop the M50's mechanism, as Marines found out to their cost in Guadalcanal, and the Reising guns were rejected by the military and passed to non-combat security personnel and police in the USA itself. The only differences between the M50 and M55 were that the latter was designed for airborne use, having a wire stock and pistol grip (instead of a wooden butt) and no compensator.

SPECIFICATIONS

COUNTRY OF ORIGIN USA
CALIBRE .45in M1911
LENGTH 787mm (31in) stock extended; 570mm (22.5in) stock folded
WEIGHT 2.89kg (6.37lb)
BARREL 266mm (10.5in), 6 grooves, rh
FEED/MAGAZINE CAPACITY 12- or 25-round box magazine
OPERATION Delayed blowback
MUZZLE VELOCITY 280mps (920fps)
EFFECTIVE RANGE 120m (400ft)
CYCLIC RATE OF FIRE 500rpm

SIG MP41

The SIG MP41 actually began its development life in two earlier submachine guns, the MK33 and MK37. These guns of the 1930s made little commercial impact, though they did allow SIG to experiment with different types of blowback mechanism suited to the submachine gun form. In 1941 SIG produced the MP41. This operated using a straightforward blowback system and was chambered for the 9mm Parabellum cartridge. It was solidly built, perhaps too solidly, for the receiver was made from forged steel and this combined with the extensive wooden furniture made the gun heavy to wield. Yet despite its ungainly proportions, it worked well. Thus it is more puzzling that the Swiss army preferred the problematic Furrer M41/44 as its choice of weapon, and the SIG MP41 was discontinued.

SPECIFICATIONS

COUNTRY OF ORIGIN Switzerland
CALIBRE 9mm Parabellum
LENGTH 800mm (31.5in)
WEIGHT 4.3kg (9.6lb)
BARREL 306mm (12.05in) 6 grooves, rh
FEED/MAGAZINE CAPACITY 40-round detachable box magazine
OPERATION Blowback
MUZZLE VELOCITY 400mps (1312fps)
EFFECTIVE RANGE 300m (984ft)
CYCLIC RATE OF FIRE 850rpm

Austen Mk 1

The Austen was the Australian attempt to produce a wartime submachine gun that was of better quality and reliability than the British Stens which the Australian forces were receiving from 1941. Their answer was a fusion of the Sten and the German MP40. Thus, while the barrel, receiver and trigger belonged to the Sten, the mainspring, bolt and stock are from the MP40. The combination was a successful one and the Austen proved to be a thoroughly competent weapon in action, with a greater durability than the Sten. Thus the Austen and Owen submachine guns were able to equip the Australian forces. Yet, though some 20,000 Austens were made, it was the Owen that dominated, mainly because it had a reliability that the Austen could not match.

SPECIFICATIONS

COUNTRY OF ORIGIN Australia
CALIBRE 9mm Parabellum
LENGTH 845mm (33.25in) stock extended; 552mm (21.75in) stock folded
WEIGHT 3.98kg (8.75lb)
BARREL 196mm (7.75in), 6 grooves, rh
FEED/MAGAZINE CAPACITY 28-round detachable box magazine
OPERATION Blowback
MUZZLE VELOCITY 380mps (1246fps)
EFFECTIVE RANGE 50m (164ft)
CYCLIC RATE OF FIRE 500rpm

M3A1

Like so many submachine guns of World War II, the M3 was designed specifically to meet the requirements of mass production. Designed by George Hyde and produced by General Motors, the M3 came on line in 1942 and earned the title 'Grease Gun' on account of its crude appearance. It was capable of firing both 9mm and .45 ACP calibre rounds by simple changes of bolt, barrel and magazine, but the latter calibre was by far the most popular. It fired at a relatively low 450rpm via a simple blowback mechanism and, apart from one or two problems with the straight-line magazine feed and the durability of some of its cheap pressed-steel components, it proved itself a totally serviceable weapon. The M3A1's main virtue as a gun was that it was there – 650,000 were made by 1944 – and it worked.

SPECIFICATIONS

COUNTRY OF ORIGIN USA
CALIBRE .45 ACP or 9mm Parabellum
LENGTH 762mm (30in) stock extended; 577mm (22.75in) stock folded
WEIGHT 3.7kg (8.15lb)
BARREL 203mm (8in), 4 grooves, rh
FEED/MAGAZINE CAPACITY 30-round detachable box magazine
OPERATION Blowback
MUZZLE VELOCITY 275mps (900fps)
EFFECTIVE RANGE 50m (164ft)
CYCLIC RATE OF FIRE 450rpm

Sten Mk II

The Sten Mk II was the definitive Sten gun, being the most numerous (more than two million produced) and having the crude metal construction that was the gun's visual signature. Its overall construction was even simpler than the Mk I's had been. The wooden trigger housing was replaced by a pressed steel box, and the butt, which was removable for cleaning the breech block and mainspring, now consisted of a simple metal tube and shoulder plate. The magazine port could also be turned to cover the aperture when the gun was not in use. The Sten Mk II was manufactured in the United Kingdom, Canada and New Zealand, and furnished not only regular Allied troops, but also many Resistance fighters who appreciated the way it could easily be broken down and concealed.

SPECIFICATIONS

COUNTRY OF ORIGIN UK
CALIBRE 9mm Parabellum
LENGTH 762mm (30in)
WEIGHT 2.95kg (6.5lb)
BARREL 196mm (7.75in), 2 or 6 grooves, rh Feed/
MAGAZINE CAPACITY 32-round detachable box magazine
OPERATION Blowback
MUZZLE VELOCITY 380mps (1247fps)
EFFECTIVE RANGE 70m (230ft)
CYCLIC RATE OF FIRE 550rpm

Type 100

Japan only designed one submachine gun during World War II and production began in 1942. The Type 100 was a conventional blowback weapon consistently let down by its underpowered 8mm Nambu pistol round, which had a tendency to jam. Notable features included a chrome-lined barrel and a muzzle break, while modifications included a folding-stock paratrooper's gun. Production ceased in 1943 before being restarted in 1944 with the Type 100/44. This came at a time when Japan was struggling to match the US forces' scale of firepower in the Pacific, and the Type 100's rpm was taken from 400 to 800. Despite simplifying the design, production never achieved the rate needed and most Japanese in the Pacific had to rely on rifles against the US BARs, M3s, M1s and Thompsons.

SPECIFICATIONS

COUNTRY OF ORIGIN Japan
CALIBRE 8mm Nambu
LENGTH 890mm (35in)
WEIGHT 3.83kg (8.44lb)
BARREL 228mm (9in), 6 grooves, rh
FEED/MAGAZINE CAPACITY 30-round box magazine
OPERATION Blowback
MUZZLE VELOCITY 335mps (1100fps)
EFFECTIVE RANGE 70m (230ft)
CYCLIC RATE OF FIRE 450rpm (1940); 800rpm (1944)

United Defense M42

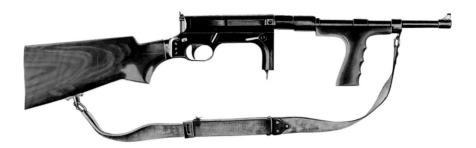

The United Defense M42 is a fine gun with an enigmatic history. It was designed by High Standard as a commercial weapon just prior to World War II and produced by Marlin to orders from the governmental United Defense Supply Corporation. The activities of this shadowy organisation are little known, but they were certainly involved in bolstering special forces and secret service activities. Thus, some 15,000 M42s went to scattered European and Far Eastern destinations, where the recipients were well served by its excellent quality of machining and finishing. It had a reliable blowback operation and a bolt handle which sealed the boltway against dirt intrusion. Despite its quality, the dominance of the Thompson guns meant the UD M42 was unable to make headway into mainstream markets.

SPECIFICATIONS
COUNTRY OF ORIGIN USA
CALIBRE 9mm Parabellum
LENGTH 820mm (32.25in)
WEIGHT 4.11kg (9.06lb)
BARREL 279mm (11in), 6 grooves, rh
FEED/MAGAZINE CAPACITY 20-round detachable box magazine
OPERATION Blowback
MUZZLE VELOCITY 400mps (1312fps)
EFFECTIVE RANGE 120m (400ft)
CYCLIC RATE OF FIRE 700rpm

PPS-43

The PPS-43 has been rather eclipsed by its more famous relative, the PPSh-41, yet it was much its equal even though the conditions of its production meant that only one million were made, as opposed to the five million PPSh-41s. The PPS-43 was designed by Sudarev and produced in Leningrad during the seige there in 1941–44. The seige meant that the gun had to be extremely simple in manufacture and this was achieved in the PPS-42 and then the marginally variant PPS-43. The PPS weapons were entirely made of sheet steel and their lightness and folding butt meant that production continued even after the seige, as they found popularity with armoured vehicle crews. Simple as it was, the PPS-43 had a long postwar life in the Korean War and also as a model for the Finnish M/1944.

SPECIFICATIONS

COUNTRY OF ORIGIN USSR/Russia
CALIBRE 7.62 x 25mm Soviet
LENGTH 889mm (35in) stock extended; 635mm (25in) stock folded
WEIGHT 3.36kg (7.4lb)
BARREL 254mm (10in), 4 grooves, rh
FEED/MAGAZINE CAPACITY 35-round detachable box magazine
OPERATION Blowback
MUZZLE VELOCITY 500mps (1640fps)
EFFECTIVE RANGE 100m (328ft) plus
CYCLIC RATE OF FIRE 650rpm

Sten Mk IIS

The Sten MkIIS was an attempt to give British and Commonwealth special forces soldiers a silenced weapon for special operations, and was particularly used by RM Commandos. On the whole it was successful, as the Mk IIS was remarkably quiet, the noise of the reciprocating bolt being louder than the actual noise of firing. The Mk IIS had an integrated barrel and silencer (thus it was a separate version of the Sten altogether) and it fired bullets at a subsonic muzzle velocity of 305mps (1000fps). It was designed for single-shot use – full-automatic could be applied but created excessive wear on the baffles in the silencer. As the silencer would become extremely hot during firing, a canvas sleeve was wrapped around it as a protective foregrip. The Mk IIS later saw service during the Korean War.

SPECIFICATIONS
COUNTRY OF ORIGIN UK
CALIBRE 9 x 19mm Parabellum
LENGTH 908mm (35.75in)
WEIGHT 3.52kg (7.76lb)
BARREL 89mm (3.5in), 6 grooves, rh
FEED/MAGAZINE CAPACITY 32-round detachable box magazine
OPERATION Blowback
MUZZLE VELOCITY 305mps (1000fps)
EFFECTIVE RANGE 50m (164ft)
CYCLIC RATE OF FIRE 450rpm

Dux

The story behind the Dux is infinitely more fascinating than the features of the gun itself, it being effectively the same as the Finnish M44, but of better quality. The match with the M44 is not coincidental. In 1944, one of the M44's designers, Willie Daugs, fled to Spain from Germany and turned his M44 design drawings over to the Orviedo Arsenal. As the result of collaboration with Ludwig Vorgrimmler, the Dux 51 was born in the early 1950s and went into service with the West German Border Police as the M53, where its use continued until the end of the 1960s. Neither the M53 nor some of the redeveloped prototypes which followed found their way into military service, mainly because of legal rather than military reasons. By the 1970s, the design was being superseded and the Dux fell into disuse.

SPECIFICATIONS
COUNTRY OF ORIGIN Germany/Spain
CALIBRE 9mm Parabellum
LENGTH 825mm (32.48in) stock extended; 615mm (24.25mm) stock folded
WEIGHT 3.49kg (7.69lb)
BARREL 248mm (9.75in), 6 grooves, rh
FEED/MAGAZINE CAPACITY 50-round box magazine
OPERATION Blowback
MUZZLE VELOCITY 390mps (1280fps)
EFFECTIVE RANGE 70m (230ft)
CYCLIC RATE OF FIRE 500rpm

Konepistooli M44

Produced as an almost direct copy of the superb Soviet PPS-43, the Konepistooli M44 was made into the Finns' own by their adapting it for 9mm Parabellum ammunition. Despite this, it had little to distinguish it from its inspiration, although its feed system was interchangeable between the 71-round Suomi drum and a 50round box magazine. It would later (mid-1950s) be modified to accept the 36-round Carl Gustav magazine, and this version was known as the M44/46. Coming from such good stock, the M44 proved a perfectly acceptable weapon. There was little to go wrong with its basic blowback system, although its lack of selector switch (it could only fire full automatic) made it seem increasingly archaic compared to the new international assault rifles and it was taken out of service in the late 1960s.

SPECIFICATIONS
COUNTRY OF ORIGIN Finland
CALIBRE 9mm Parabellum
LENGTH 825mm (32.48in) stock extended; 623mm (24.53in) folded
WEIGHT 2.8kg (6.17lb)
BARREL 247mm (9.72in), 4 or 6 grooves, rh
FEED/MAGAZINE CAPACITY 71-round drum or 50-round box magazine
OPERATION Blowback
MUZZLE VELOCITY 395mps (1300fps)
EFFECTIVE RANGE 70m (230ft)
CYCLIC RATE OF FIRE 650rpm

Patchett Mk 1

The Patchett submachine gun was the brainchild of George Patchett, and it emerged as part of the British forces' attempt to develop a more satisfying replacement for the crude Sten gun. Prototypes of the weapon were produced by the Sterling Armament Co. during 1942–1943 (in 1942, Sterling had stopped making the Lanchester). These guns were promisingly tested in combat conditions during the British airborne assault at Arnhem and production of the Mk 1 started in 1944. The Patchett had a solid design and a durable blowback mechanism, and was improved to form the Patchett Mk 2, which in turn became the famous Sterling submachine gun. The main difference between the Patchett and the Sterling is that the former used a straight magazine box and could accept Sten magazines.

SPECIFICATIONS
COUNTRY OF ORIGIN UK
CALIBRE 9mm Parabellum
LENGTH 685mm (27in)
WEIGHT 2.7kg (6lb)
BARREL 195mm (7.75in), 6 grooves, rh
FEED/MAGAZINE CAPACITY 32-round detachable box magazine
OPERATION Blowback
MUZZLE VELOCITY 395mps (1295fps)
EFFECTIVE RANGE 70m (230ft)
CYCLIC RATE OF FIRE 550rpm

Sten Mk V

By 1944, when the Sten Mk V appeared, the war had turned in the Allies' favour and a little more time and effort could be lavished on the Sten's initially crude design. The Mk V was basically the same Sten as ever in terms of operation and, crucially, feed system. The latter was significant because the Sten's magazine was the root of its unreliability; thus the Mk V carried forward that unreliability. Yet the Mk V was undoubtedly better in a cosmetic sense. It now had a wooden stock (in early models, this featured a trap for holding gun-cleaning equipment), pistol grip and, again in early models, a forward grip which was eventually dropped because it kept breaking off. It also had the muzzle and fore-sight of the Lee-Enfield No. 4 rifle and could take that rifle's bayonet.

SPECIFICATIONS
COUNTRY OF ORIGIN UK
CALIBRE 9mm Parabellum
LENGTH 762mm (30in)
WEIGHT 3.86kg (8.5lb)
BARREL 196mm (7.75in), 6 grooves, rh
FEED/MAGAZINE CAPACITY 32-round box magazine
OPERATION Blowback
MUZZLE VELOCITY 380mps (1247fps)
EFFECTIVE RANGE 70m (230ft)
CYCLIC RATE OF FIRE 600rpm

Carl Gustav M/45

Built for the Swedish Army in the immediate aftermath of World War II, the Kulspruta Pistol M/45 (as it is formally known – the Carl Gustav title relates to the factory where it was produced) is an automatic-fire, blowback weapon which is well machined and known for its reliability and durability. These qualities took it into service with the US special forces during the Vietnam War, when it was fitted with an integral silencer, and Indonesia and Egypt have also become major customers (the latter making the Carl Gustav under licence as the 'Port Said'). The stability of the original design has meant that modifications have been minimal and the current 9mm round is claimed by Sweden to be the most powerful submachine gun round available.

SPECIFICATIONS
COUNTRY OF ORIGIN Sweden
CALIBRE 9mm Parabellum
LENGTH 808mm (31.81in) stock extended; 552mm (21.73in) stock folded
WEIGHT 3.9kg (8.6lb)
BARREL 213mm (8.38in), 6 grooves, rh
FEED/MAGAZINE CAPACITY 36-round box magazine
OPERATION Blowback
MUZZLE VELOCITY 410mps (1345fps)
EFFECTIVE RANGE 120m (400ft)
CYCLIC RATE OF FIRE 600rpm

MAT 49

The MAT 49 was developed by Manufacture d'Armes de Tulle just after World War II; the company's designers were asked to design a standardised French submachine gun. Made from the most basic processes of stamping and limited machining, the MAT 49 is nonetheless a sound weapon. Its reliability proved itself in the wars in French Indochina and throughout Africa and Southeast Asia in France's former colonies. Indeed, many police and military units still rely on the gun today, although French forces now have the 5.56mm FAMAS rifle as their standard issue. Two interesting features of the MAT 49 are the hinged magazine housing which folds underneath the barrel for storage/carriage, and the way in which the chamber actually wraps around the bolt on firing, rather than the other way round.

SPECIFICATIONS
COUNTRY OF ORIGIN France
CALIBRE 9mm Parabellum
LENGTH 720mm (28.35in) stock extended; 460mm (18.11in) stock folded
WEIGHT 3.5kg (7.72lb)
BARREL 228mm (8.98in), 4 grooves, rh
FEED/MAGAZINE CAPACITY 20- or 32-round box magazine
OPERATION Blowback
MUZZLE VELOCITY 390mps (1280fps)
EFFECTIVE RANGE 70m (230ft)
CYCLIC RATE OF FIRE 600rpm

Madsen M50

The Madsen M50 was actually one of a series of guns made by Dansk Industri Syndikat AS Madsen immediately after WWII. The series was initiated by the disappointing M45, but truly established itself with the M46. This blowback weapon borrowed design and production techniques from the British Sten, US M3 and the Russian PPS guns, the result being a simple, serviceable weapon. Non-standard features, however, included a pressed steel receiver which was hinged and, with the barrel removed, could be opened up to inspect the gun's internal mechanism. The M50 differed from the M46 only marginally – the cocking handle was changed so that it did not have to be removed during stripping, but it was actually one of the most successful guns of the range.

SPECIFICATIONS

COUNTRY OF ORIGIN Denmark
CALIBRE 9 x 19mm Parabellum
LENGTH 800mm (31.5in) stock extended; 530mm (20.85in) stock folded
WEIGHT 3.17kg (6.99lb)
BARREL 197mm (7.75in), 4 grooves, rh
FEED/MAGAZINE CAPACITY 32-round detachable box magazine
OPERATION Blowback
MUZZLE VELOCITY 380mps (1274fps)
EFFECTIVE RANGE 150m (492ft) plus
CYCLIC RATE OF FIRE 550rpm

Maxim .45 Mk 1

Maxim's ground-breaking machine guns entered active service with the British Army in the late 1800s, and were soon proving their military value in action in Britain's African colonies. The first gun to be adopted by the British was designated 'Gun, Maxim, 0.45in, Mk 1'. This was first calibrated for the heavy .455in calibre round that was also used in the Martini-Henry breech-loading rifle, then in the Royal Navy's 0.45in Gardner-Gatling round, but in 1889 a .303in version was established and this became the norm (though .45in guns would continue in service until 1915). The 0.303in round was awkward for Maxim in that he struggled to get enough recoil to operate the automatic action, though the change to a cordite propellant solved much of that problem.

SPECIFICATIONS
COUNTRY OF ORIGIN UK
CALIBRE .303in British
LENGTH 1180mm (46.5in)
WEIGHT 18.2kg (40lb)
BARREL 720mm (28.25in), 4 grooves, rh
FEED/MAGAZINE CAPACITY Belt feed
OPERATION recoil, water cooled
MUZZLE VELOCITY 600mps (1970fps)
EFFECTIVE RANGE 2000m (6561ft)
CYCLIC RATE OF FIRE 600rpm

8mm Saint-Etienne Modèle 1907

The Saint-Etienne Modèle 1907 (M'le'07) was a disastrous machine gun based on the equally ineffective earlier gun, the M'le'05 'Puteaux'. A textbook lesson in how to create an overcomplex, unreliable weapon, the M'le'07 reversed the gas-piston operation of its forebear to a forward direction, thus requiring a rack-andpinion system to push the bolt backwards. This unnecessary complexity was compounded by the return spring being directly beneath the barrel, where the spring was weakened by the barrel's heat drawing the temper from the steel. Such problems made it a precarious weapon to use in dirty environments (i.e. the entire Western Front) and it was removed from service. Its one interesting feature was that adjustments could be made to the gas cylinder to vary the rate of fire.

SPECIFICATIONS
COUNTRY OF ORIGIN France
CALIBRE 8 x 50R Lebel
LENGTH 1180mm (46.5in)
WEIGHT 25.75kg (57lb)
BARREL 710mm (28in), 4 grooves, rh
FEED/MAGAZINE CAPACITY 24- or 30-round metallic strip
OPERATION Gas, air-cooled
MUZZLE VELOCITY 700mps (2300fps)
EFFECTIVE RANGE 2000m (6600ft)
CYCLIC RATE OF FIRE 500rpm

Schwarzlose M07/12

The Schwarzlose machine guns used a delayed-blowback action, in which the breech block was operated by breech pressure alone. This necessitated a high block weight and a toggle system which retarded recoil until the pressure reached levels safe enough to open the breech. The need to control pressure also led to a short barrel (the round had to leave the muzzle before breech opening), so effective range was comparatively limited at around 1000m (3300ft). Yet the range was capable enough and the gun entered service with the Austro-Hungarian Army in 1905 and several other European armies during the pre– and post–WWI periods. It emerged in four main designs, the most popular of which was the M07/12, which could also be chambered for both 7.92mm German and 6.5mm Dutch calibres.

SPECIFICATIONS

COUNTRY OF ORIGIN Austria
CALIBRE 8 x 56R Austrian Mannlicher
LENGTH 1070mm (42in)
WEIGHT 20kg (44lb)
BARREL 525mm (20.75in), 4 grooves, rh
FEED/MAGAZINE CAPACITY 250-round cloth belt
OPERATION Delayed blowback, water-cooled
MUZZLE VELOCITY 618mps (2030fps)
EFFECTIVE RANGE 1000m (3300ft) plus
CYCLIC RATE OF FIRE 425rpm

Maxim Maschinengewehr '08

With the Vickers machine gun, the Maxim '08 dominated the landscape of the Western Front during World War I. Like the previous weapons developed by Hiram Maxim in the late 1890s, the '08 was a short-recoil gun which used a toggle system in breech locking and was water cooled. The '08 became the foremost frontline machine gun of German forces during World War I; a single gun could produce dependable fire for hour after hour at 450rpm when fitted with a muzzle booster to increase recoil force. The one drawback of the '08 was its mounted weight – 62kg (136.69lb) with its sledge mounting – and the subsequent '08/15 replaced the sledge with a bipod and shoulder stock which reduced overall weight to little more than 18kg (39.68lb).

SPECIFICATIONS

COUNTRY OF ORIGIN Germany
CALIBRE 7.92 x 57mm Mauser
LENGTH 1175mm (46.25in)
WEIGHT 26.44kg (58.29lb)
BARREL 719mm (28.3in), 4 grooves, rh
FEED/MAGAZINE CAPACITY 250-round belt
OPERATION Short recoil, water-cooled
MUZZLE VELOCITY 892mps (2925fps)
EFFECTIVE RANGE 2000m (6600ft) plus
CYCLIC RATE OF FIRE 300–450rpm

Spandau Model 1908/15

While the Maxim 08/15 was performing well on the ground, a different version was required for the expanding role of air combat during WWI. This, the Model 1908/15, was produced initially by the Spandau Arsenal and was often termed the Light Maxim. It was a conventional recoil-type Maxim, identifiable by its heavily ventilated cooling jacket which allowed effective barrel cooling when on an aircraft mount. However, the Light Maxim often had a higher rate of fire than the heavy version on account of a muzzle booster being used to increase recoil speed. Though the Spandau gun was mounted on many Fokker Eindeckers, it actually found more application as a land weapon, and after the war many were recalibrated and adapted back to water-cooling for a medium machine gun role.

SPECIFICATIONS
COUNTRY OF ORIGIN Germany
CALIBRE 7.92 x 57JS
LENGTH 1397mm (55in)
WEIGHT 14.96kg (33lb)
BARREL 711mm (28in) 4 grooves, rh
FEED/MAGAZINE CAPACITY Belt feed
OPERATION Recoil
MUZZLE VELOCITY 892mps (2925fps)
EFFECTIVE RANGE 2000m (6600ft) plus
CYCLIC RATE OF FIRE 550rpm

Hotchkiss Mk 1

As machine guns became in increasing demand during WWI, the British decided to manufacture the Hotchkiss Mle 1909 under licence in the .303in British calibre and relabelling it '0.303in Gun, Machine, Hotchkiss, Mk 1'. Essentially, the British gun was the same as the French original, but with several significant improvements to aid its function and deployment. Most important was the replacement of the central tripod on the French gun with a butt and a bipod. This gave the gun a much greater ease of application as a light machine gun. The strip feed, however, was still unsatisfactory, so, from mid-1917, the Mk 1* gun was issued. This was capable of switching between strip and belt feed (although the latter was actually composed of three-round strips linked together).

SPECIFICATIONS
COUNTRY OF ORIGIN UK
CALIBRE .303in British
LENGTH 1187mm (46.73in)
WEIGHT 12.25kg (27lb)
BARREL 596mm (23.5in), 4 grooves, rh
FEED/MAGAZINE CAPACITY 30-round metal strip, or belt feed (three-strip links)
OPERATION Gas, air-cooled
MUZZLE VELOCITY 739mps (2425fps)
EFFECTIVE RANGE 1000m (3300ft)
CYCLIC RATE OF FIRE 500rpm

Skoda M1909

In 1888, Major George Ritter von Dormus and Archduke Karl Salvator won patents for a distinctive delayed-blowback gun, the delay provided by a pivoting block and large coil spring housed in the receiver. Following several models, the M1909 was a competitive response to the more efficient Schwarzlose machine guns produced within Austria. Its rate of fire was improved by the addition of an oiling system for the cartridge belt feed and the removal of the pendulous rate reducer which had previously kept fire to a maximum of 250rpm. The M1909 was belt-fed from a 250-round cartridge belt, as opposed to earlier gravity-fed models, but the overall inefficiencies of the series were never overcome and, after one more variation, the M1913, Skoda ceased machine gun production.

SPECIFICATIONS

COUNTRY OF ORIGIN Austria-Hungary
CALIBRE 8 x 50R Austrian Mannlicher
LENGTH 1070mm (42in)
WEIGHT 44kg (20lb)
BARREL 525mm (20.75in)
FEED/MAGAZINE CAPACITY 250-round fabric belt
OPERATION Delayed blowback, water-cooled
MUZZLE VELOCITY 618mps (2030fps)
EFFECTIVE RANGE 1000m (3300ft) plus
CYCLIC RATE OF FIRE 425rpm

Maxim MG1910

Maxim guns spread across the world either through supply or licensed manufacture. The MG1910 was the second of Russia's Maxim productions (the first being the MG1905) and was effectively a Maxim MG'08, with some modifications. Most of the improvements were concentrated into the feed mechanism which was made out of sheet steel and featured a large filling aperture at the top through which water, snow and other coolants could be quickly applied. The gun pictured here is on the standard Sokolov wheeled mount, a mount which also allowed horizontal firing action via a turntable. By mid–World War II, the Maxim was being replaced by the Goryunov SG43, but the MG1910's service history lasted well into the Cold War in many developing countries.

SPECIFICATIONS

COUNTRY OF ORIGIN USSR/Russia
CALIBRE 7.62 x 55R Soviet
LENGTH 1107mm (43.6in)
WEIGHT 9.12kg (20.1lb)
BARREL 605mm (23.8in), 4 grooves, rh
FEED/MAGAZINE CAPACITY 250-round fabric belt
OPERATION Short recoil, water-cooled
MUZZLE VELOCITY 863mps (2830fps)
EFFECTIVE RANGE 1100m (3608ft)
CYCLIC RATE OF FIRE 550rpm

Vickers Mark 1 (Class C)

The .303 Vickers was a British improvement on the Maxim gun that became one of the most successful machine guns of all time. The improvements made included reduced weight through using high-quality steel and aluminium, a dramatically shortened receiver achieved by inverting break direction in the Maxim toggle lock system, and improved feed. The Vickers entered service with the British Army in 1912 and proved a reliable, powerful weapon which endured in production until 1945 and combat into the 1960s and beyond. The Mark I was the first of the Vickers series; the subsequent models were mostly mounting variations for air or armour use. Regardless of weather or conditions, the Vickers could maintain heavy fire for long periods, only let down in its early period by faulty ammunition.

SPECIFICATIONS

COUNTRY OF ORIGIN UK
CALIBRE .303in British
LENGTH 1155mm (40.5in)
WEIGHT 18kg (40lb)
BARREL 723mm (28.5in), 4 grooves, rh
FEED/MAGAZINE CAPACITY 250-round fabric belt
OPERATION Recoil, water-cooled
MUZZLE VELOCITY 600mps (1970fps); later 730mps (2400fps)
EFFECTIVE RANGE 2000m (6600ft)
CYCLIC RATE OF FIRE 600rpm

Perino M1913

The Perino M1913 was Italy's first attempt to match the Maxim. The original gun was designed by Giuseppe Perino and patented in 1900, yet received little interest due to its excessive weight which could exceed 25kg (55.12lb). It was only with the 1913 version that the weight was reduced to 13.65kg (30lb). In other regards, however, the Perino had several salient features. Using the 6.5mm rifle cartridge, it operated through a mix of recoil and gas. Its barrel was cooled by a piston-like configuration which enclosed the barrel and pumped in cool air when the barrel was in oscillation under firing. Like many early Italian guns, its feed system tended towards over-complexity. It went from a chain feed contained in a drum to a stack magazine system with five trays holding 12 rounds each.

SPECIFICATIONS

COUNTRY OF ORIGIN Italy
CALIBRE 6.5mm M95
LENGTH 1180mm (46.5in)
WEIGHT 13.65kg (30lb)
BARREL 655mm (27.75in)
FEED/MAGAZINE CAPACITY Magazine feed
OPERATION Combined gas/recoil, water-cooled
MUZZLE VELOCITY 740mps (2428fps)
EFFECTIVE RANGE 1500m (4950ft)
CYCLIC RATE OF FIRE 500rpm

Fiat-Revelli Modello 14

The Modello 14 was one of Italy's first home-grown machine guns. An unusual and over-machined weapon, it served until 1945. Using the limited force of the 6.5mm M95 rifle cartridge, it had a delayed blowback operation and every round was oiled from a reservoir on top of the receiver to aid extraction (the oil attracted dust and caused stoppages). Behind the recoiling breech was an external buffer rod which impacted at 400 cycles per minute on a pad only inches from the firer's hands. This made it a fearsome weapon to use, while the tendency for cartridges to split under pressure in the chamber also made it prone to stoppages. Another distinctive feature was the feed: 10 clips of rifle ammunition set in a 10-compartment drum, a clip being fed in before the magazine revolved to the right and dropped in the next clip.

SPECIFICATIONS

COUNTRY OF ORIGIN Italy
CALIBRE 6.5 x 52mm M95
LENGTH 1180mm (46.5in)
WEIGHT 17kg (37.75lb)
BARREL 645mm (25.75in), 4 grooves, rh
FEED/MAGAZINE CAPACITY 50-round strip-feed box
OPERATION Gas, air-cooled
MUZZLE VELOCITY 640mps (2100fps)
EFFECTIVE RANGE 1500m (4950ft)
CYCLIC RATE OF FIRE 400rpm

Hotchkiss Mle 1914

Hotchkiss & Co. are credited with producing the world's first viable gas-operated machine gun in 1895. This gun spawned an evolving series of weapons which ultimately equipped French, Greek, British and US forces during World War I; the Mle 1914 actually became the standard light machine gun for the French Army during that conflict. Previous Hotchkiss guns were fed by the 24- or 36-round rigid metallic strip, yet the Mle 1914 worked with what was effectively a belt feed created by linking three-round strips into a 249-round belt. The Mle 1914 proved to be a reliable weapon, although, like its predecessor, the Mle 1909, was too heavy for the mobile infantry use for which it was intended. After the war, a 7mm version was produced which opened export markets in Mexico, Spain and Brazil.

SPECIFICATIONS

COUNTRY OF ORIGIN France
CALIBRE 8mm Lebel
LENGTH 1270mm (50in)
WEIGHT 23.6kg (52lb)
BARREL 775mm (30.5in), 4 grooves, lh
FEED/MAGAZINE CAPACITY 24- or 30-round metallic strip or 249-round strip/belt
OPERATION Gas, air-cooled
MUZZLE VELOCITY 725mps (2380fps)
EFFECTIVE RANGE 2000m (6600ft) plus
CYCLIC RATE OF FIRE 600rpm

Parabellum MG14

As military aircraft improved, so the demand for aircraft-mounted weaponry expanded. The Maxim '08 was too heavy for airborne use, so the engineering company Deutsche Waffen und Munitionsfabrik (DWM) was commissioned to design a lighter weapon. The Parabellum machine gun appeared in 1911 and utilised the same upward toggle break mechanism used by the Vickers machine gun and Parabellum pistol. It was very successful in its intended role, with a high rate of fire and good reliability. The MG14 was the dominant incarnation and was applied to a flexible aircraft mount in aircraft or, in a water- (as opposed to air-) cooled version, in Zeppelin airships. Towards the end of WWI, the MG14 appeared in a ground-fire role in 1918 (with a thinner barrel jacket), where it performed equally well.

SPECIFICATIONS

COUNTRY OF ORIGIN Germany
CALIBRE 7.92 x 57mm Mauser
LENGTH 1225mm (48.25in)
WEIGHT 9.8kg (21.5lb)
BARREL 726mm (28.5in), 4 grooves, rh
FEED/MAGAZINE CAPACITY 200-round metal link belt
OPERATION Recoil, air-cooled
MUZZLE VELOCITY 890mps (2920fps)
EFFECTIVE RANGE 2000m (6600ft) plus
CYCLIC RATE OF FIRE 600rpm plus

Taisho 3

The redoubtable Hotchkiss weapons of the early 20th century were models for many a nation's machine-gun development, not least Japan's. Hotchkiss Mle 1900s made significant combat impact when used by Japanese soldiers during the Russo-Japanese War of 1904–1905 and inspired the designer Kirijo Nambu to create a similar weapon for Japanese production. Chambered for the 6.5mm Arisaka rifle cartridge, the Taisho 3 went into service in 1914 and was in most ways a simple Hotchkiss copy, although visually it was distinguished by its tripod system and the extensive use of broad cooling fins along the length of the barrel to dissipate heat. The tripod was unique in that holes sited on the tripod feet accepted poles that enabled the gun to be lifted intact by a single team.

SPECIFICATIONS

COUNTRY OF ORIGIN Japan
CALIBRE 6.5 x 50mm Arisaka
LENGTH 1155mm (45in)
WEIGHT 28kg (62lb)
BARREL 749mm (29.5in), 4 grooves, lh
FEED/MAGAZINE CAPACITY 30-round metal strip
OPERATION Gas, air-cooled
MUZZLE VELOCITY 731mps (2400fps)
EFFECTIVE RANGE 1500m (4950ft)
CYCLIC RATE OF FIRE 400rpm

Fusil Mitrailleur M'15 ('Chauchat')

This cheap, roughly produced and unreliable weapon has earned itself the title of the worst machine gun in history from some authorities. The accusation seems sustainable. Known commonly as the 'Chauchat', after the commission that brought it into service, its long-recoil system was entirely unsuitable for its relatively low weight: the barrel and bolt recoiled for the full stroke before the barrel returned to its firing position (known as its 'battery') and then the bolt released itself, extracting the spent cartridge and chambering the new round. This violent action was hard to control, as was the Chauchat's tendency to jam owing to the poor quality and ill adjustment of many of its components. Used by France, Belgium and Greece during World War I, it was a precarious and hated weapon on which to rely in combat.

SPECIFICATIONS

COUNTRY OF ORIGIN France
CALIBRE 8 x 50R Lebel
LENGTH 1145mm (45in)
WEIGHT 9kg (20lb)
BARREL 469mm (18.5in), 4 grooves, rh
FEED/MAGAZINE CAPACITY 20-round box magazine
OPERATION Recoil, air-cooled
MUZZLE VELOCITY 700mps (2300fps)
EFFECTIVE RANGE 1000m (3300ft) plus
CYCLIC RATE OF FIRE 250rpm

7.92mm Bergmann MG15

The Bergmann MG15 was the WWI production version of the earlier MG10, brainchild of Theodor Bergmann and Louis Schmeisser. Like many weapons in the history of German gun production, it was somewhat ahead of its time, using a modern aluminium-link belt-feed system and a short-recoil operation. Initially water cooled, it was superseded during the war by the air-cooled MG15Na (the previous water jacket was replaced by a slotted metal barrel surround) which featured a pistol grip and trigger, a recoil pad fitted to the rear of the receiver, a tripod mounting and a drum magazine to contain the belt. The MG15Na was a fine gun which served until the 1930s, but the dominance of the Maxim '08 during the war meant that it never acquired much enthusiasm from military officials.

SPECIFICATIONS

COUNTRY OF ORIGIN Germany
CALIBRE 7.92 x 57mm Mauser
LENGTH 1120mm (44in)
WEIGHT 12.9kg (28.5lb)
BARREL 726mm (28.5in), 4 grooves, rh
FEED/MAGAZINE CAPACITY 200-round metal-link belt
OPERATION Recoil, air-cooled
MUZZLE VELOCITY 890mps (2925fps)
EFFECTIVE RANGE 2000m (6600ft) plus
CYCLIC RATE OF FIRE 500rpm

Lewis Gun Mk 1

The Lewis gun is named after US Army Colonel Isaac Newton Lewis, even though he actually did little more than perfect a design by the physician and weapons designer Samuel McClean. Yet, having had the gun rejected by the US Army, Lewis took it to Europe where it was adopted by the Belgian Army in 1913 and manufactured under licence in Britain from 1914 by the BSA company. (The US Army, as a consequence of its decision to reject the Lewis, went to war with the abysmal French Chauchat instead.) Despite the intrigues and acrimony of its origins, the Lewis gun was a fine weapon with many superb innovations. Gas operated, the Lewis had a rotating-bolt system driven by the gas piston itself and was cooled via a system of fins between the muzzle and barrel casing which drew cool air into the jacket through the air current set up by the muzzle blast, although this added to the gun's overall weight, and was later found

SPECIFICATIONS

COUNTRY OF ORIGIN UK
CALIBRE .303in British Service and others
LENGTH 965mm (38in)
WEIGHT 11.8kg (26lb)
BARREL 666mm (26.25in), 4 grooves, lh
FEED/MAGAZINE CAPACITY 47- or 97-round drum
OPERATION Gas, air-cooled
MUZZLE VELOCITY 745mps (2444fps)
EFFECTIVE RANGE 1000m (3300ft) plus
CYCLIC RATE OF FIRE 550rpm

to have little effect. In its most common form, the Lewis Mk I, it fired either drum magazines of either 47 or 97 rounds of .303 ammunition. It proved itself as a dependable gun in both world wars.

Browning M1917A1

The Browning name is legendary in the history of machine-gun development, and the M1917 started one of the finest series of firearms to date. Developed in the days prior to World War I, the .30 M1917 (so titled after its adoption date by the US Army) had much in common with Maxim guns in its water-cooled, recoil-operated configuration. The Browning was produced by several manufacturers during World War I (Remington, Colt and Westinghouse) and 68,000 were made for wartime service. The M1917A1 was a postwar (1936) revision of the weapon and differed in features of feed mechanism, sight graduation and tripod. Many other variations followed, all of which built upon the reliability and toughness of the original weapon. The M1917 was not replaced by air-cooled weapons until the late 1950s.

SPECIFICATIONS
COUNTRY OF ORIGIN USA
CALIBRE .30in M1906
LENGTH 980mm (38.5in)
WEIGHT 15kg (32.75lb)
BARREL 610mm (24in), 4 grooves, rh
FEED/MAGAZINE CAPACITY 250-round fabric belt
OPERATION Recoil, water-cooled
MUZZLE VELOCITY 850mps (2800fps)
EFFECTIVE RANGE 2000m (6600ft) plus
CYCLIC RATE OF FIRE 500rpm

Browning M1919A4

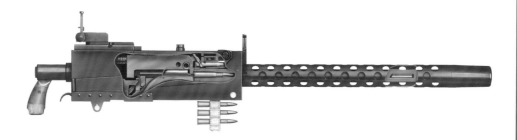

By the end of WWI a new Browning was on the drawing board as an air-cooled replacement for the water-cooled M1917 which had given stalwart service on the Western front. This gun was known as the M1919, just too late to be put into active service. It would, however, take its place as one of the definitive weapons of the 20th century. The first model (M1919A1) was intended for use on armoured vehicles, but later models were designed for the cavalry (M1919A2), a general-purpose weapon (M1919A3) and finally an infantry version, the M1919A4. This latter gun became the prevalent form, and serves US and worldwide forces to this day. The basic M1919 configuration was a short-recoil, fabric or metal link belt fed weapon which was strong, reliable, easily controlled and capable of sustained suppressive fire beyond ranges of 2000m (6561ft). Over 438,000 M1919A4s were issued by 1945. They were used in a whole host of different roles, including

antiaircraft, aircraft-mounted and vehicle-mounted capacities. The 1943 M1919A6 was lighter with a butt, bipod and carrying handle, but it was never really popular.

SPECIFICATIONS

COUNTRY OF ORIGIN USA
CALIBRE .30in Browning
LENGTH 1041mm (41in)
WEIGHT 14.05kg (31lb)
BARREL 610mm (24in), 4 grooves, rh
FEED/MAGAZINE CAPACITY 250-round fabric or metal-link belt
OPERATION Recoil operated, air cooled
MUZZLE VELOCITY 853mps (2800fps)
EFFECTIVE RANGE 2000m (6561ft) plus
CYCLIC RATE OF FIRE 50rpm

Browning M2HB

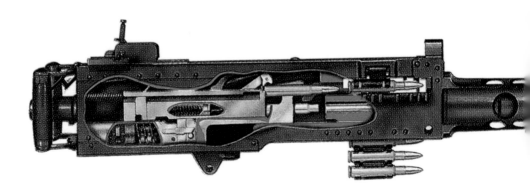

Famous the world over for the sheer
power of its .50 calibre (12.7mm)
round, the Browning M2HB ('Heavy
Barrel') emerged from the US Army's
request in 1918 for a more potent weapon
with which to attack enemy vehicles and
aircraft. Browning's initial answer was the
water-cooled M1921 (a M1917 modified
to accept Winchester's new .50 cartridge),
which in the 1930s became the M2
air-cooled weapon. The cartridge's power
meant that the barrel could overheat after
only 75 rounds of constant firing, so a
heavy barrel was added to dissipate heat
and this became the dominant model,

the M2HB. Apart from numerous changes
to mounts and other components, the
M2HB used today is essentially the same
as the original. More than three million
have been produced and used by the
world's armies.

SPECIFICATIONS

COUNTRY OF ORIGIN USA
CALIBRE .50in Browning
LENGTH 1655mm (65in)
WEIGHT 38.5kg (84lb)
BARREL 1143mm (45in), 8 grooves, rh
FEED/MAGAZINE CAPACITY 110-round metallic-link belt

OPERATION Recoil, air-cooled
MUZZLE VELOCITY 898mps (2950fps)
EFFECTIVE RANGE 3000m (9900ft) plus
CYCLIC RATE OF FIRE 450–550rpm

Hotchkiss M1922/26

The M1922/26 was one of several Hotchkiss models which emerged in the interwar period. On paper, several elements of the M1922/26 were promising. It had standard gas operation, but the rate of fire could be reduced through a regulator in front of the trigger. It could accept three types of feed: top-mounted magazine, the side-fed Hotchkiss metal strip or the Hotchkiss metal-link belt consisting of three-round strips joined together. The muzzle also had a climb compensator fitted. Yet the immediate aftermath of WWI was not a good time for many weapons manufacturers, and Hotchkiss struggled to make a profit. The Greek Army took some 5000 (as the M/1926) in 6.5 x 54mm Mannlicher calibre and lesser quantities went out (in 7mm calibre) to countries in South and Central America.

SPECIFICATIONS

COUNTRY OF ORIGIN France
CALIBRE 6.5mm Mannlicher and others
LENGTH 1215mm (47.75in)
WEIGHT 9.5kg (21lb)
BARREL 575mm (22.75in), 4 grooves, rh
FEED/MAGAZINE CAPACITY 25- or 30-round metal strip
OPERATION Gas, air-cooled
MUZZLE VELOCITY 745mps (2444fps)
EFFECTIVE RANGE 1000m (3300ft) plus
CYCLIC RATE OF FIRE 500rpm

Taisho 11

World War I and the interwar years saw increased global interest in the concept of the light machine gun as an easily transportable infantry weapon; the Taisho 11 was Japan's first production of this type. It came into service in 1922 and saw action until 1945. It had several distinguishing features, such as sights offset to the right of the muzzle and receiver, and, in particular, its 30-shot, oil-lubricated hopper feed system. This ran on six clips of the same 6.5mm ammunition used in the Arisaka 38 rifle, each round being individually stripped from the clip and fed into the breech. Thus, if the machine gunner's ammunition ran out, any rifleman could provide theirs for use. The feed system was not the most reliable, however, and the oil lubrication system was problematic when dust invaded.

SPECIFICATIONS

COUNTRY OF ORIGIN Japan
CALIBRE 6.5 x 50mm Arisaka
LENGTH 1105mm (43.5in)
WEIGHT 10.2kg (22.5lb)
BARREL 482mm (19in), 4 grooves, rh
FEED/MAGAZINE CAPACITY 30-round hopper
OPERATION Gas, air-cooled
MUZZLE VELOCITY 760mps (2500fps)
EFFECTIVE RANGE 1500m (4950ft)
CYCLIC RATE OF FIRE 500rpm

Fusil-mitrailleur Modèle 1924 M29

The M'le 24 was France's positive escape in the late 1920s from the hideous deficiencies of the Chauchat. The awkward rimmed 8mm Lebel cartridge was replaced with a rimless 7.5mm round which fed more easily. Recoil operation gave way to gas operation, based on the US BAR (Browning Automatic Rifle). The M'le 1924 worked fairly well, although some modifications were required to the cartridge type, when the gun was redesignated the M'le 1924/29 Châtellerault, after its place of development. Produced between 1930 and 1940, it served until the 1950s and was the French Army's standard light machine gun during WWII. A static defence version for the Maginot Line featuring a 150-round side-mounted drum magazine was known as the M'le 1931, which was also used on French armour.

SPECIFICATIONS

COUNTRY OF ORIGIN France
CALIBRE 7.5 x 54mm M29
LENGTH 1080mm (42.5in)
WEIGHT 9.25kg (20.25lb)
BARREL 500mm (19.75in), 4 grooves, rh
FEED/MAGAZINE CAPACITY 25-round box magazine
OPERATION Gas, air-cooled
MUZZLE VELOCITY 825mps (2700fps)
EFFECTIVE RANGE 1000m (3300ft) plus
CYCLIC RATE OF FIRE 500rpm

SIA

Italy has produced many fine handguns and submachine guns, but its history of light and heavy machine gun manufacture is less distinguished. The SIA (Societa Anonima Italiana G. Ansaldo, Armstrong & Co.) light machine gun was produced in the 1920s and let down by several less than satisfactory features. Its delayed blowback mechanism was not the most reliable, while the magazine had an open top and bottom which only served to input dirt into the SIA's vulnerable workings and to make extraction unpredictable. However, the gun also contained some ingenuity. This included fluting the chamber gas flowing between the chamber wall and the cartridge case, which stopped the case from sticking under the firing pressure. The SIA ended up as a training weapon for the Italian Army in the 1930s.

SPECIFICATIONS

COUNTRY OF ORIGIN Italy
CALIBRE 6.5 x 52mm Carcano
LENGTH Not available
WEIGHT 10.66kg (25.3lb)
BARREL Not available
FEED/MAGAZINE CAPACITY 25-round metal strip
OPERATION Delayed blowback
MUZZLE VELOCITY 645mps (2116fps)
EFFECTIVE RANGE Not available
CYCLIC RATE OF FIRE 700rpm

Degtyarev DP

The Degtyarev DP was a characteristically tough Russian weapon and, from 1928, its subsequent variants would stay in production until the 1950s. Its gas operation and locking system (which had locking flaps applied by the forward movement of the firing pin) were very simple and the gun offered reliability even in the filthiest of conditions. The DP was, however, slightly let down by its most prominent visual feature – its 42-round drum magazine. The flat drum was necessary to feed the awkward rimmed 7.62mm Soviet round successfully, and it could be easily damaged. Also, the gas-piston spring, being positioned underneath the barrel, was weakened over time by the heat drawing the temper out of the spring steel. Despite these problems, the DP was a strong addition to the Soviet arsenal.

SPECIFICATIONS

COUNTRY OF ORIGIN USSR/Russia
CALIBRE 7.62 x 54R Soviet
LENGTH 1290mm (50.8in)
WEIGHT 9.12kg (20.1lb)
BARREL 605mm (23.8in), 4 grooves, rh
FEED/MAGAZINE CAPACITY 47-round drum magazine
OPERATION Gas, air-cooled
MUZZLE VELOCITY 840mps (2760fps)
EFFECTIVE RANGE 2000m (6600ft)
CYCLIC RATE OF FIRE 500–600rpm

Type 89

The Type 89 was a Japanese aircraft gun which found itself mounted within a variety of naval and army fighters in the Pacific theatre. Its design speaks of the tendency of Japan during WWII to copy Vickers and Browning designs and because of this, the Type 89 was one of the better weapons in Japan's arsenal at this time. It was usually mounted in pairs and was a capable gun in strafing and range-finding roles, though the latter activity was its dominant – once the pilot had ascertained target range using the Type 89 he would usually revert to his heavier cannons for the attack. Because range-finding required long, sustained bursts of fire at the target, the Type 89 was built to last, and it had a particularly heavy barrel to help disperse heat during rapid fire.

SPECIFICATIONS

COUNTRY OF ORIGIN Japan
CALIBRE 7.7mm
LENGTH 1051mm (41.4in)
WEIGHT 16.78kg (37lb)
BARREL 685mm (27in) 4 grooves, rh
FEED/MAGAZINE CAPACITY Fabric belt
OPERATION Recoil
MUZZLE VELOCITY Not available
EFFECTIVE RANGE 2000m (6600ft) plus
CYCLIC RATE OF FIRE 600 rpm plus

Fucile Mitragliatore Breda M30

The Modello 30 was one of the new breed of light machine guns that emerged from Italy in the interwar period and was an over-investment in design that came unstuck in practicality. Apart from the fact that the quick-change barrel was slightly pointless without a changing handle, the gun's defining feature was its feed system. This consisted of an integral box which was hinged on the right side of the receiver. Loading consisted of opening the box, filling it with rifle chargers, then locking it back into place. Theoretically, the design had the advantage of having more effective and dependable feed than a detachable box; however, in practice, if the magazine was damaged, the gun was useless. Add its oil-assisted extraction method and its general ungainliness, and the Modello 30 was not a great success.

SPECIFICATIONS

COUNTRY OF ORIGIN Italy
CALIBRE 6.5 x 52mm M95 and others
LENGTH 1230mm (48.5in)
WEIGHT 10.2kg (22.5lb)
BARREL 520mm (20.5in), 4 grooves, rh
FEED/MAGAZINE CAPACITY 20-round integral box magazine
OPERATION Blowback, air-cooled
MUZZLE VELOCITY 610mps (2000fps)
EFFECTIVE RANGE 1000m (3300ft)
CYCLIC RATE OF FIRE 475rpm

Lehky Kulomet ZB vz30

The Lehky Kulomet ZB vz30 was an improved version of the superb vz26. It became the eventual model for the British Bren gun after the test centre staff at Enfield could scarcely find enough superlatives to describe its performance during trials. Like the vz26, it boasted an incredibly smooth action by virtue of the long gas cylinder (which slowed the rate of fire and impressively reduced the ferocity of recoil), and its quick-change barrel and great accuracy made it popular with troops. The main differences in the vz30 from the vz26 were modifications to the firing-pin and breech-block mechanism. Both Britain and Germany produced versions of it during WWII, the German weapon being known as the MG30(t); in either its original or licensed forms, it has been produced from Spain to China.

SPECIFICATIONS
COUNTRY OF ORIGIN Czechoslovakia
CALIBRE 7.92mm Mauser and others
LENGTH 1160mm (45.75in)
WEIGHT 9.6kg (21.25lb)
BARREL 627mm (24.7in), 4 grooves, rh
FEED/MAGAZINE CAPACITY 30-round box magazine
OPERATION Gas, air-cooled
MUZZLE VELOCITY 762mps (2500fps)
EFFECTIVE RANGE 1000m (3300ft) plus
CYCLIC RATE OF FIRE 500rpm

Solothurn MG30

The MG30 was Solothurn's second product under the control of Rheinmetall. Though it did not achieve a great success in itself – only about 5000 were made during the 1930s – the configuration it established acted as the foundations for two of the greatest machine guns of all time, the MG34 and MG42. This heritage is visually recognisable in the MG30's straight-in-line arrangement between butt and and barrel. The MG30 had some interesting features. It was recoil-operated, worked from a side-mounted magazine, and it had a quick-change barrel facility which was operated by twisting the butt and withrawing both barrel and bolt out from the receiver. Its curious-looking rocker trigger enabled the user to fire both single shots by pulling the top section and full automatic by depressing the lower section.

SPECIFICATIONS

COUNTRY OF ORIGIN Germany
CALIBRE 7.5 x 54mm Schmidt rubin
LENGTH 1175mm (46.25in)
WEIGHT 7.7kg (17lb)
BARREL 595mm (23.42in), 4 grooves, rh
FEED/MAGAZINE CAPACITY 25-round detachable box magazine
OPERATION Recoil operated, air cooled
MUZZLE VELOCITY 800mps (2650fps)
EFFECTIVE RANGE 2000m (6561ft) plus
CYCLIC RATE OF FIRE 500rpm

Type 92

Nicknamed 'the woodpecker' by Australians who faced its stuttering fire in the Pacific, the Type 92 was issued in 1932 and signalled a shift in the Japanese Army from using the 6.5mm Arisaka round to a more potent semi-rimless 7.7mm cartridge, which increased muzzle velocity by around 32mps (100fps). The 7.7mm cartridge inexplicably came in rimmed and semi-rimmed varieties. While the rimmed cartridge would not feed through the Type 92, the other cartridges could be used without interchange modifications – although a subsequent 1941 version, known as the Type 1, could only accept the Type 99 rimless round. Apart from the ammunition, slight modifications in breech and barrel, and freedom from the need for cartridge belt oiling were all that distinguished the Type 92 from the Taisho 3.

SPECIFICATIONS

COUNTRY OF ORIGIN Japan
CALIBRE 7.7mm Type 92/Type 99
LENGTH 1160mm (45in)
WEIGHT 55kg (122lb)
BARREL 700mm (27.5in), 4 grooves, rh
FEED/MAGAZINE CAPACITY 30-round metal strip
OPERATION Gas, air-cooled
MUZZLE VELOCITY 715mps (2350fps)
EFFECTIVE RANGE 2000m (6600ft)
CYCLIC RATE OF FIRE 450rpm

MG34

The MG34 was one of the finest machine guns of the 20th century, and effectively introduced the concept of the general purpose machine gun. It was designed to function both in assault roles using a bipod, and sustained roles on a tripod or vehicular mounting, and it excelled in both. It was also mounted as an anti-aircraft gun. The MG34 could fire at 800–900rpm, could easily be stripped simply by twisting out the barrel and was totally controllable in firing owing to the 'in-line' design which placed aligned barrel and butt horizontally. Its success took it into service as the standard German army machine gun in 1936, and it held this title until supplanted by the MG42. The reason for its replacement was purely one of cost – the MG34 was exhaustively machined and proved too expensive.

SPECIFICATIONS

COUNTRY OF ORIGIN Germany
CALIBRE 7.92 x 57mm Mauser
LENGTH 1219mm (48in)
WEIGHT 12.1kg (26.67lb)
BARREL 627mm (24.75in), 4 grooves, rh
FEED/MAGAZINE CAPACITY 250-round belt
or 75-round saddle drum

OPERATION Recoil-operated, air-cooled
MUZZLE VELOCITY 762mps (2500-fps)
EFFECTIVE RANGE 2000m (6600ft) plus
CYCLIC RATE OF FIRE 800–900rpm

Fiat-Revelli Modello 35

The Fiat-Revelli Modello 35 (M1935) was Italy's attempt to improve on the overt complexities of the Modello 14, but the result was actually to create increased unreliability and danger to the user. Out went the under-powered 6.5mm cartridge and in came an 8mm round, the chamber being fluted (grooves cut into its surface to equalise pressure inside and outside the cartridge) to cope with the power increase and dispense with the lubricating reservoir. An air-cooled system replaced the water-cooled predecessor and a standard belt feed was fitted. All these improvements were undone by major design and safety flaws. The gun fired from a closed-bolt position, which in this case led to overheating and 'cooking off' – the spontaneous firing of heated rounds. After 1945, the M1935 was scrapped.

SPECIFICATIONS

COUNTRY OF ORIGIN Italy
CALIBRE 8 x 59RB
LENGTH 1270mm (50in)
WEIGHT 19.5kg (43lb)
BARREL 680mm (26.75in), 4 grooves, rh
FEED/MAGAZINE CAPACITY 50-round belt
OPERATION Gas, air-cooled
MUZZLE VELOCITY 790mps (2600fps)
EFFECTIVE RANGE 2000m (6600ft)
CYCLIC RATE OF FIRE 450rpm

BESA

In the years leading up to and during World War II, the United Kingdom purchased two weapons from Czechoslovakia for production: the ZB26, which became the Bren gun, and the ZB53, which was the BESA when manufactured by Birmingham Small Arms (BSA) Co. The BESA was intended purely for mounting on armoured vehicles. It was gas operated, with a progressive differential recoil system in which the round was fired while the breech block was moving forwards; the discharge arrests the travel and shortens it, thus greatly reducing recoil. The BESA was thus a very accurate weapon. From the Mark 1 BESA, the gun ran through several variations; most significantly, the Mark 1 and Mark 2 had a rate selector to vary the rpm, while the Mark 3 was fixed at the high rate of fire and the Mark 3* at the low.

SPECIFICATIONS

COUNTRY OF ORIGIN Great Britain/Czechoslovakia
CALIBRE 7.92mm Mauser
LENGTH 1105mm (43.5in)
WEIGHT 21.5kg (47lb)
BARREL 736mm (29in), 4 grooves, rh
FEED/MAGAZINE CAPACITY 225-round belt
OPERATION Gas, air-cooled
MUZZLE VELOCITY 825mps (2700fps)
EFFECTIVE RANGE 2000m (6600ft) plus
CYCLIC RATE OF FIRE 750–850rpm

Bren

A remarkable testament to the Bren Gun's quality is that it is still used by the British Army today as the Bren Gun L4A2 (in 7.62mm NATO). The Bren originated from a series of trials in the 1930s for a replacement for the outdated Lewis. The winner was the Czech 7.92mm vz.27, adapted at the Royal Small Arms Factory at Enfield Lock to take the British rimmed .303 catridge. The result was the 'Bren', a compound of Brno, its place of origin in Czechoslovakia, and Enfield. The Mark I was a superb gun to handle, accurate and easy to maintain. Subsequent models speeded up production through simplification, but never lost the quality of the firearm. There were essentially five versions of the .303in Bren before the introduction of the 7.62mm L4 weapons. The original Mk 1 initially had a pistol grip situated beneath the gun's butt for the gunner's free hand. This, however, was not popular and was quickly removed as production increased.

SPECIFICATIONS
COUNTRY OF ORIGIN UK
CALIBRE .303in British
LENGTH 1150mm (45.25in)
WEIGHT 10.25kg (22.5lb)
BARREL 625mm (25in), 6 grooves, rh
FEED/MAGAZINE CAPACITY 30-round box magazine
OPERATION Gas-operated, air-cooled
MUZZLE VELOCITY 730mps (2400fps)
EFFECTIVE RANGE 1000m (3300ft) plus
CYCLIC RATE OF FIRE 500rpm

While the Bren did not have the same rpm and range of the German MG34 and MG42, its accuracy was exceptional owing to a very light recoil, and it was a superb support weapon.

Type 96

The Type 96 was designed as the successor to the Taisho 11, but it was not produced in sufficient numbers to supplant the latter and both saw service until 1945. Most of the Type 96's improvements over the Taisho 11 were concentrated in the feed mechanism. The cartridge oiler system was (unwisely) retained, but, instead of being located on the gun itself, it was fitted into the 30-round box magazine, itself an improvement over the Taisho 11's hopper-feed system. In addition, barrel change was made quicker. These modifications, however, were not enough to free the gun from many of the irregularities of performance and accuracy of its predecessor. Strange, therefore, that a telescopic sight was designed for the gun, as it was scarcely of value considering the capabilities of the gun.

SPECIFICATIONS
COUNTRY OF ORIGIN Japan
CALIBRE 6.5 x 50mm Arisaka
LENGTH 1055mm (41.5in)
WEIGHT 9kg (20lb)
BARREL 555mm (21.75in), 4 grooves, rh
FEED/MAGAZINE CAPACITY 30-round box magazine
OPERATION Gas, air-cooled
MUZZLE VELOCITY 730mps (2300fps)
EFFECTIVE RANGE 1000m (3300ft)
CYCLIC RATE OF FIRE 550rpm

DShK

Varieties of the DShK are still in use today around the world and nearly 50 years in production testifies to the basic soundness of its design. It was developed as a heavy machine in the early 1930s and was in demand on the Eastern Front during World War II as the DShK-38 (the number refers to year of modification). This gun used a complex rotary-feed system which was dropped after the war in favour of standard flat-feed. Although the gun itself was a good piece of engineering, the intentional weight reductions over previous Soviet machine guns were somewhat lost through its excessively heavy infantry carriage, although this could also become an anti-aircraft tripod. The DShK found its true home on armoured vehicles, especially tank turrets, and it reaches towards the Browning M2HB in performance.

SPECIFICATIONS

COUNTRY OF ORIGIN USSR/Russia
CALIBRE 12.7mm Soviet
LENGTH 1586mm (62.5in)
WEIGHT 35.5kg (78.5lb)
BARREL 1066mm (42in), 4 grooves, rh
FEED/MAGAZINE CAPACITY 50-round belt
OPERATION Gas, air-cooled
MUZZLE VELOCITY 850mps (2788fps)
EFFECTIVE RANGE 2000m (6600ft) plus
CYCLIC RATE OF FIRE 550rpm

BESAL Mk II

The little-known BESAL was the product of British fears during WWII that the bombing of the Royal Small Arms Factory at Enfield would severely disrupt Bren gun production. As a contingency measure, BSA were commissioned to design a low-budget version of the Bren which could be made in any reasonably equipped engineering plant if need be – the BESAL Mk I. The simplification brief was rigorously achieved: steel pressings replaced machining; the breech block and piston were of square section; the gun was cocked by pulling back the pistol grip; sights and bipod were limited to double and fixed positions, respectively. Yet, due to the soundness of the Bren design and the BESAL designer's ingenuity, the weapon performed well and would have proved a decent substitute had the need arose.

SPECIFICATIONS
COUNTRY OF ORIGIN UK
CALIBRE .303in
LENGTH 1185mm (46.75in)
WEIGHT 9.75kg (20.5lb)
BARREL 558mm (22in), 4 grooves, rh
FEED/MAGAZINE CAPACITY 30-round box magazine
OPERATION Gas, air-cooled
MUZZLE VELOCITY 730mps (2300fps)
EFFECTIVE RANGE 1000m (3300ft)
CYCLIC RATE OF FIRE 600rpm

Rolls Royce MG

Rolls Royce has had a fine name in the defence industry for many years, though not in the field of weapons manufacture. The Rolls Royce machine gun which emerged in the 1940s was therefore somewhat of an exception. The development of the gun can be seen in the context of experimentations in very heavy calibre machine guns that several British arms manufacturers conducted in the 1930s. While Vickers produced a .50in calibre machine gun and BESA a 15mm weapon, Rolls Royce went on to produce a prototype heavy machine gun for use by troops and on armoured vehicles. While a solid gun using a Friberg/Kjellman type of breech-locking system and having a range of around 3000m (9842ft) the Rolls Royce MG stayed as a prototype and Rolls Royce kept its focus elsewhere.

SPECIFICATIONS

COUNTRY OF ORIGIN UK
CALIBRE .50in M2
LENGTH 1270mm (50in)
WEIGHT 22.25kg (49lb)
BARREL 1020mm (40in)
FEED/MAGAZINE CAPACITY Belt feed
OPERATION Recoil operated, air cooled
MUZZLE VELOCITY 715mps (2350fps)
EFFECTIVE RANGE 3000m (9828ft)
CYCLIC RATE OF FIRE 1000rpm

MG42

The MG42 emerged in 1941 from Germany's desperate need to speed up the process of machine gun manufacture over that of the superb, but expensive and intricate, MG34. Mauser took up the challenge in 1940, and looked to the new production methods that were already pumping out weapons such as the MP40 submachine gun. The MG42's production advantage was that it used processes of metal stamping and welding instead of machining on the receiver and barrel housing, processes which dramatically increased output. Yet the changes were not all relegated to production processes. A superb new locking system was introduced, using two locking rollers which cammed outwards to recesses on the receiver walls, and a quick-change barrel facility made the gun very popular with users. The result was a light, accurate, functional machine gun with a very high rate of fire which produced a curious rasping sound likened to tearing linoleum.

SPECIFICATIONS

COUNTRY OF ORIGIN Germany
CALIBRE 7.92 x 57mm Mauser
LENGTH 1220mm (48in)
WEIGHT 11.5kg (25.35lb)
BARREL 535mm (21in), 4 grooves, rh
FEED/MAGAZINE CAPACITY 50-round belt
OPERATION Short recoil operated, air cooled
MUZZLE VELOCITY 800mps (2650fps)
EFFECTIVE RANGE 3000m (10,000ft) plus
CYCLIC RATE OF FIRE 1200rpm

It first appeared in Africa and Russia in 1942 and soon became a source of fear for Allied troops. A variant of the MG42, the MG45, was curtailed by the end of World War II.

Goryunov SGM

The Goryunov SGM was a variant of an earlier Soviet medium machine gun, the Goryunov SG43. This had been produced in the early 1940s to replace the Maxim MG1910. The SG43 used features such as a tilting breech-block locking system and, despite an awkward feed system because of the rimmed rounds, the gun's performance was dependable. Its reliability stemmed from factors such as its very solid construction, a quick-change barrel and a chromium-plated bore. The SGM was one of a string of variants produced during WWII. Little was different to the SG43: the SGM featured a fluted barrel and a cocking handle fitted beneath the receiver. In turn, the SGM was adapted for tank use (the SGMT) and also made in a version with protective covers for its ejection and feed apertures (the SGMB).

SPECIFICATIONS

COUNTRY OF ORIGIN USSR/Russia
CALIBRE 7.62 x 54R Soviet
LENGTH 1120mm (44.1in)
WEIGHT 13.6kg (29.98lb)
BARREL 719mm (28.3in), 4 grooves, rh
FEED/MAGAZINE CAPACITY 250-round belt
OPERATION Gas, air-cooled
MUZZLE VELOCITY 850mps (2788fps)
EFFECTIVE RANGE 1000m (3300ft)
CYCLIC RATE OF FIRE 650rpm

Ithaca Model 37 M and P

The Ithaca 37 series of shotguns is not a range of commercial guns that have simply stepped into military and police use – they are purpose-designed for these specialist roles. Ithaca 37 guns served in World War II and have kept their popularity, even, it is rumoured, amongst special forces soldiers. Most prevalent today is the Ithaca 37 M and P ('Military and Police'), a 12-gauge shotgun which comes in two barrel lengths – 470mm (18.5in) and 508mm (20in) – and has either a five- or an eight-round tubular magazine. Another model, the charmingly-named DS ('Deerslayer'), has similar specifications, but has a barrel engineered to fire heavy slugs when necessary. The DS led to the Model LAPD, a special gun with modified sights and furniture, and improved carrying straps and sling swivels for specific police use.

SPECIFICATIONS
COUNTRY OF ORIGIN USA
CALIBRE 12
LENGTH 1016mm (40in) for 508mm barrel
WEIGHT 2.94kg (6.48lb) or 3.06kg (6.75lb)
BARREL 470mm (18.5in) or 508mm (20in)
FEED/MAGAZINE CAPACITY 5- or 8-round integral tubular magazine
OPERATION Pump action
MUZZLE VELOCITY Variable, depending on type of ammunition
EFFECTIVE RANGE 100m (328ft)

Index